Mistakes Were Made

Andy C Wareing

Andy C Wareing

Copyright © 2023 Andy C Wareing All rights reserved

No part of this book may be reproduced, or stored in a retrieval system, or transmitted in any form or by any means, electronic, mechanical, photocopying, recording, or otherwise, without express written permission of the publisher.

Cover design by Andy C Wareing

All rights reserved.

ISBN- 9798587678491

Contents

Dedication	v
1. We will always have Paris	1
2. Hawaii	3
3. Hawaii Again	6
4. Changes	9
5. Espana	12
6. Ship or Sell	18
7. New Horizons	21
8. Portents	23
9. Pandemic	25
10. Shady Grove	28
11. A Window of Opportunity	30
12. A Farewell	33
13. Leaving the USA	35
14. An English Quarantine	39
15. Escape	42
16. An Evening with Henry	47
17. Viva Espana	50
18. Arrival	55

19. First Day	59
20. Life in Spain	62
21. More life in Spain	68
22. Even more life in Spain	71
23. Perpignan	75
24. Sennely	78
25. A Return to Paris	81
26. Southport	85
27. Second Quarantine	87
28. Somerset	90
29. New Horizons	92
Andy C Wareing	96

To our dearest friend, always sorely missed...
Alyn Nash

We Will Always Have Paris

July 30th, 2020

 The needle on the temperature gauge of the aging Ford Mondeo crept relentlessly, dangerously once more into the red, and the car slowed dangerously. Blistering steam began to rise from the engine compartment in front of us. I pumped the gas pedal as we began to lose power and in the rear-view mirror, I could see a purple slick of coolant bleeding onto the searing asphalt behind us. With no air conditioning in the car, Paris was an unseasonable sweltering ninety degrees Fahrenheit. The car was packed, stacked high, and loaded with all of our earthly possessions including our two dogs who panted, hot, and distressed in the rear of the vehicle. We had all been overheated, sweating, and tense in the confines of the roasting cramped car for hours.

 Progress en-route to Paris that morning had been good, but as we approached the crossing of the Seine on the Boulevard Peripherique Est, south of the city, the lanes had narrowed, and traffic had slowed inexorably to a stop, with the exception of the endless belligerent discord of scooters and motorcycles who flew past on both sides of the stationary traffic at suicidal speeds. We had to get off this road. If the car broke down here, we would be stranded, in real trouble.

 There are no emergency breakdown lanes on the Peripherique, but the next exit was a hundred yards ahead, so with more indignant Parisian horns and vulgar hand gestures aimed at our last-minute maneuver we cut across lanes, away from the highway gridlock and parked, half in, half out in a tiny parking space on the Rue Barbes in sight of the Moulin de la Tour.

 Hot, tired, and stressed, Paula and I were at our lowest point right at that moment. We were close to despair, the two of us alone in this foreign country, seemingly stranded with the bonnet up, volumes of steam still billowing from the engine compartment, and coolant hissing onto the pavement.

The engine was slowly cooling but even if the car started it was clearly going to overheat again. The entirety of the crowded Peripherique of Paris lay between us and the long drive North to Calais, and then the train across the channel back to England that still awaited us.

At that moment it was a challenge to conceive that only six weeks ago we had still been safe in the soft and easy comfort of the United States. We had left one life, motivated to pursue the promise of a dream in Spain, but a global pandemic had been a growing and spreading shadow alongside us. From the moment we had left the US we had been forced to react to the changing whims of international governments, the overnight closing of international borders, virus hotspot popups, and rapidly emerging quarantine zones as we battled across Europe.

Around us, the sun that drifted through the leafy poplars dappled the hot tarmac of Boulevard Rue Barbes. The midday heat had brought out the office workers, young, carefree, and elegant they strolled across the street to the nearby Boulangerie Au Vieux Moulin from where the smell of sweet pastries and freshly baked bread drifted. They looked in our direction, exchanged amused glances and raised hands to mouths to whisper then walked away smirking, pleased that they didn't share our predicament.

Paula asked me if I wanted her to walk across the road to buy a pastry while we waited for the car to cool. I could only shake my head no. My mouth was a desert, dry with trepidation at how we could possibly get ourselves out of this situation. A gendarme, dressed in black and wearing his Kepi, appeared from around the corner across the road from us. He paused to stare at us intently, badly parked as we were. He wore a mustache and struck an uncanny resemblance to Officer Crabtree from the British TV series 'Allo, Allo.'

He began to walk in our direction and my heart sank even further, by this time it was languishing somewhere between my knees and the pavement. Allo Allo is a TV comedy about a small French town and its occupants living through World War II in German-occupied France, and Officer Crabtree is an English secret agent masquerading as a French policeman. He believes he can speak fluent and flawless French, but badly mangles every vowel. And as he walked across, I suspected we were soon about to be up shots crick without a piddle.

Hawaii

September 2017

Douglas Adams wrote, "Nothing travels faster than the speed of light with the possible exception of bad news, which obeys its own special laws."

Hawaii was 4,500 miles and a six-hour time difference from Atlanta where we lived at that time, but bad news had easily navigated both distance and time zones to meet us there on the two occasions we had had the otherwise good fortune to visit.

Our first vacation was to Maui in September of 2017. We woke early, ready and excited for a trip up the ten-thousand-foot-high Haleakala crater and subsequent twenty-three-mile bicycle descent. On our already sun-drenched balcony overlooking the ocean, I stretched and yawned and checked my phone to make sure our youngest son, Adam, who was dog-sitting at home, hadn't left me a message overnight.

My phone and Facebook page were filled with rumors of the death of Alyn, one of my closest friends and work colleagues. Alyn was a quirky but very talented single guy, originally from the United Kingdom where we started working in the software industry together. He was far smarter than me and had somehow managed to escape that particular rat race and moved to become a snowboard instructor at Big White in Canada. A few years later and with Alyn needing some additional finances, and me missing a skilled resource on the West Coast, I had gladly and recently recruited him back to work with me in the States and things couldn't have been going better. Then, suddenly and overnight, at only forty-seven, he had got dehydrated and exhausted, mountain biking at altitude near his home in Kelowna Canada, and simply passed out, never to revive.

Alyn was an adventurer, not a thrill-seeker, but someone who cherished life and sought out and embraced any new experience. He was superbly deficient in whatever sequence of DNA that codes for fear, the primeval lizard sense of self-preservation that makes most of us stop dead, ice water in our veins, reconsidering that next imprudent course of action.

He told me once he was excited to be going Heliskiing at the weekend, taking a helicopter with some friends to the top of some distant snowy peak, far beyond the reach of ski lifts and the capabilities of most mortals, and then descending on virgin and near-vertical off-piste trails. I asked him on Monday how it had gone, "didn't get there," was his despondent reply. Assuming the weather had grounded the helicopter, I asked him why. Turned out the helicopter *had* taken off, but at a few thousand feet had ascended through the fog and experienced supercooling conditions, icing the rotor blades, adding weight and drag, and forcing the helicopter to make an emergency landing into a snowbank. I tried to explain the difference between "not getting there" and a "crash landing" but the subtlety was completely lost on him.

He was also funny as hell without even knowing it. I was seated next to Alyn, only a few weeks prior, in another bullshit corporate training event, tedious as usual. We had just finished lunch and I was sipping on a diet Coke. Alyn leaned across to whisper.

"Man, we had a crappy weekend, took the dogs and some friends to a scenic spot overlooking Lake Kalamalka for a picnic."

I leaned in so we didn't disturb the class and whisperingly asked why it hadn't worked out.

"The place was full of snakes, snakes everywhere, snakes under every rock, snakes crawling in the grass, really dangerous for the dogs so we had to leave".

I took another sip of coke and told him it sounded scary and asked him what the place was called.

"Rattlesnake Point," he responded drily, making me snort diet coke and emit a cough to suppress laughter, silencing the class and drawing irate looks our way.

As a snowboard instructor, he reveled in teaching kids. One day out on the slopes with nine or ten young skiers, he explained the importance of knowing what to do should one of them have an accident. He patiently told them all to mark the scene of the accident by placing their skis and poles uphill of the victim in an "X" shape. The next day one of the ski patrol saw a bunch of kids standing in a circle, mid-slope with their poles and skis crossed. Thinking one of the kids had fallen or got into difficulties, the snow patrol zoomed across the slope in their snowmobile. When they got there, they found Alyn completely sparked out, legs and arms akimbo, like some red-robed snow angel, surrounded by his class. He had attempted a Frontside 360 but mistimed it and struck his head, striking what little sense remained from his cranium.

And now, overnight...he was gone. It seemed inconceivable that Alyn, younger and much fitter than me, a boxer, a runner, a snowboard instructor, somebody universally adored by everybody, could simply, overnight, cease to exist. We tried to celebrate my fifty-third birthday on the beach on the last day of that trip in Hawaii, but a cloud, dark and somber had appeared on the horizon.

The sudden loss threw into sharp relief the ephemeral and random, haphazard nature of life and sparked much personal introspection about my own work-life balance. It lit a tiny ember of possibility regarding the future potential of me getting out of the rat race of corporate America.

Hawaii Again

August 2019

The decision to look closely into retirement came after our second Hawaii trip, soon after our Delta flight from Atlanta to Honolulu touched down on a Friday afternoon on one of the last few days of August 2019. We had one more flight to complete our eleven-hour long journey to Kauai where we would vacation for the next seven days, this time accompanied by Adam, so the three of us headed to the Kona Brewing bar in the terminal for a quick Longboard lager or two to shake off the cobwebs. Seated with a cold beer and phone in hand I checked messages, the phone pinged and the text read simply, "Tony has been let go."

I had worked with Tony for the last fourteen years, ever since I did an intra-company transfer from the UK to the US, and we were both Vice President level in a billion-dollar software company. We worked really closely together and had a decent friendship. The company making him redundant was shockingly sudden, unforeseen, and sadly predictable. Back at work, there were many other changes and job losses, but my role seemed to be safe, at least for the time being.

For the greater part, corporate America is relentless in its demand for loyalty from its employees, while displaying none towards them, and the folks from the bottom, almost to the top, have largely bought into the myth that if you put the company before all else it will value and reward you for life.

I was fortunate enough to run a team that spanned South America, the USA, Canada, Indonesia, and Glasgow. Judging by daily absences, life for the Scottish team seemed to be one long, cold and rainy, shortbread and thistle-filled holiday. And ten thousand miles distant, nobody seemed to know where the lads in Jakarta were from one single day to the next. Meanwhile, back in the good 'ole USA I couldn't for the life of me get any of the Americans to use *any* of their vacation days.

There was an all-pervading culture of pride in working longer hours than their colleagues and most of them finished up the year with a glut of vacation days. The US human resources department even created a scheme that allowed employees to donate unused days to a company-nominated charity. It is a uniquely American concept; as Christmas beckoned, you could actually hear people brag in the corridors about the size of their charitable paid time off contributions. Rather than spend time unwinding with family, they chose instead to give that gift away. When it came to *my* precious annual leave as I was always slightly less philanthropic than Scrooge McDuck. I took it all.

And what a vast difference exists in countries as pertains to statutory access to paid vacation and public holidays. Mexico offers thirteen paid vacation days, the United Kingdom provides its employees with twenty-eight days, and Indonesia provides its workers with twenty-seven days. But even better, after six years of employment, Indonesian employees are entitled to an entire month's worth of leave in their seventh and eighth years. I only had six employees in Jakarta and out of any given week at least one of them was out of the office enjoying themselves and spending time with their families. Little wonder that I barely got to know their names, never mind getting around to actually seeing them.

Let's, for a moment, compare that to the USA. Most large companies do provide paid time off, typically ten days after one year of service, rising slowly to twenty days after devoting the better part of your entire working life to them. But here is the rub, out of all of the industrialized nations on the planet, the USA actually has zero statutory agreements for paid time off. None. Not a single day is mandated by federal or state legislature.

The same with parental leave, Indonesia provides all mothers with three months at full pay, the UK provides up to an entire year for the mother to stay home with her infant, with the first thirty-two weeks paid at 90% of full pay and the same guaranteed job to return to. I had one lady who worked in Glasgow who, by pure coincidence, happened to be out on maternal leave at the time I took over management of the team. Nearly a year later her face popped up on a Zoom call and I had literally no idea who she was, or that she did in fact work for me. The reason for the salary cost discrepancies I had been scratching my head over for twelve months was solved immediately.

The United States? Nothing, nada, zilch, not a day provided to allow the mother to relax, recover, and care and bond with her newborn. Any time taken is unpaid unless you are fortunate enough for your employer to provide it as part of your package.

Amidst working in that culture, the smoldering barbeque briquette of early retirement was fanned into a small flickering flame, and then suddenly burst into a raging conflagration when I lost three male friends to suicide over the next few short weeks. All the guys were unrelated other than they all knew me. One I still worked with, one was a Tennis coach and one was an old friend from the UK. What they had in common was the exact same profile. All were middle-aged men, all successful in their chosen businesses, all surrounded by loving spouses and children who adored them. These guys were essentially me but with much, much better kids.

The decision to leave corporate America was made for me. I was done. Life was too short and far too precious to waste it working in a corporate system underpinned by a culture driven by greed, where stress, long hours, and days away from home were the norm, but loyalty was a one-way street.

But what to do next, and perhaps more importantly, with our personal healthcare tied to the employment I no longer wanted, was the United States the right place to take that next step?

CHANGES

September 2019

My wife Paula had always had a hazy dream of a life in Spain. At that point in time, we had been married twenty-eight years and had known each other pretty much our entire lives. We weren't childhood sweethearts, the conclusion that so many people jump to when they find out that we have known each other since kindergarten; we had nonetheless gone all through junior and high school together and loosely kept in touch through the subsequent years.

One night out drinking with some of my mates, I saw her at the bar of the Windmill Arms, in our hometown of Southport in England where we had both grown up. We started chatting, but she was with some other guy, clearly penniless and lacking in both looks and IQ, so we only exchanged a few pleasantries.

We started dating a few days after this reunion when I finally plucked up the courage to pick up the home phone. It was the late 1980's so the phone had a rotary dial and a curly cord that tethered it to the wall in the hall. With my Mum, Dad, and older brother all listening, amused, into the discomfort and potential rejection, I asked for a date. She agreed and I thought the first date couldn't have gone better, but when I called for a second, she tried to get her dad, John, to give me the elbow. John was the salt of the earth and luckily for me wouldn't act on her behalf.

I still struggle, after all these years, to think why Paula showed such hesitancy. I was twenty-two. Perhaps a little on the scrawny side, I did need to wear milk-bottle thick glasses that were so large they covered most of my acned face and magnified my eyes owl wide. I was doubly blessed by a scalp that refused to grow hair, by the age of seventeen I was already prematurely balding with what little hair that remained growing straight out, Einstein-like from my scalp. Come to think of it, I literally had nothing but wildly misplaced self-confidence and dogged persistence on my side, what on earth was such a beauty doing with such a loser?

Nevertheless, we bought our first little house together a year or so later using a buy high sell low methodology we still rely on for investments today, and then married a few years later. We had two sons, Ben was born in 1992 and then Adam in 1995. We had discussed emigration over the years, usually after a beer or two, Canada perhaps, or even Australia. I worked as a presales engineer in the UK at that time, visiting customers and prospects up and down the country, constantly on the road, driving over one hundred thousand miles every year, and I was desperately in need of a change of pace and scenery.

Both our parents had sadly passed within the last few years and with nothing else stopping us from looking seriously into a move to another country, we decided to go for it. When I spoke to my management team the company was broadly supportive and first offered Japan. We considered that would be too much of a challenge culturally for the kids, and their next offer was the United States. We picked Atlanta because it was the location of the company's largest office and we had one friend there. As 2006 faded into 2007, we sold our house in the UK moved the family, two dogs, and a cat to the United States, and settled in Roswell just north of Atlanta.

There is nothing trifling about an international move even to somewhere as seemingly familiar as America. The language is similar for sure, even if the spelling leaves something to be desired, but culturally America is a very foreign country. It took a lot of time and effort to adjust and adapt to the crippling bureaucracy immigrants face when, despite having the means to buy a house with cash, we had zero credit rating and no social security numbers. Every interaction was difficult for the first few months, living without standing in any computer database. Of course, it gets easier, we received our SSNs and with a few utility bills being paid regularly and on time, our credit improved. Within a few short months, our mailbox was overflowing with offers of American Express credit cards of every hue.

It's not just the organizations you have to interact with as a foreigner that are different. Americans are quite different socially from the British. Meet somebody new over a game of tennis and invite them around the house for a drink and the average American will be a no-show. Say the same to a Brit and you had better want to spend some considerable time in that person's company. They will be knocking on your front door within the hour, shouldering a party keg of warm beer, and probably won't leave until dawn. That's not to say we didn't make friends, we really did, some of the best, and ones we will always treasure, it's just subtly different.

The boys got good-naturedly teased at school initially. Atlanta is a melting pot, quite cosmopolitan by US standards, but drive north a little, to Roswell say, and it quickly becomes Georgia Southern. The British accent was a boon for me, I hammed it up no end, a veritable cast member from Downton Abbey, my plummy tones granting me twenty extra IQ points on every call I joined. For Ben and Adam not so much, the other kids constantly asking them to say "bar-nar-nar" or "bot-l of waw-tuh." They survived just fine, made good friends, and put down roots after high school. Ben joined the US Navy as a helicopter mechanic on aircraft carriers, and at the time of writing is deployed on the USS Reagan in Japan. Adam lived with us at home at the time and worked multiple jobs in retail and as a barista in local coffee shops.

Now we were back discussing another international move, this time to Spain. Spain had never been an option when I was working, but now with the kids grown, independent, and settled, and me in search of the next stage in life it seemed like a good option to explore. Three thousand miles closer to the UK where we still had friends and lots of family, brothers, sisters, nieces, and nephews. With great cost-effective health care, lots of cheap budget airlines taking Brits backward and forwards to the sun-filled resorts of the Mediterranean, and with an overall cost of living forty percent cheaper than the United States, it actually started to sound like a marvelously compelling option.

Back at work in September 2019, but now with an eye on the door, I began to seriously look at finances and what savings and investments we would be able to call on. We would never live like kings, but we had both worked hard our entire lives, and lived a life mostly free of finance and debt, and if we were careful in a country as cheap to live as Spain, at least on paper it looked like we could eke out a happy existence in the endless sunshine. When I returned home from work that day and told Paula that her dream could become a very real reality she wanted to pack up and go the next day. The decision made, we now had to figure out the logistics of the move, and more importantly, where in Spain we would live.

Only two trifling things stood in our way. We had never actually been to Spain and we didn't speak a single word of the language other than Hola!

ESPAÑA

November 2019

And so it was, in the fading light of an Atlanta evening in early November, after a couple of cold Stellas at the bar of the international departure terminal at Hartsfield Jackson airport, we boarded and settled in for the nine-hour red-eye to Manchester. The plane was typically crowded with the usual mix of weary business travelers heading to Europe, and toast-colored Brits on their way home from sun-filled vacations. Landing through the bumpy and familiar rain-burdened clouds of Manchester, we breakfasted on bacon sandwiches in the arrival's hall and then took the Trans-Pennine train through the cloudy, gloomy grey but magnificent Lake District, and arrived under cover of the glass vaulted concourse of Glasgow Central Station, the busiest train station in Scotland.

As well as the folks I managed in the US, I also had a small team based in Glasgow, so we would combine this Spanish sightseeing tour with a business trip to visit the team, some of whom were, for a change, not on vacation. The office is located in the village of Inchinnan on the outskirts of Glasgow. During World War One the art deco building was originally an airship factory but is now a beautifully renovated suite of offices filled with software developers. I was in a jet-lagged and weary state when I met the team, but with business taken care of, Paula and I took them all out for dinner that evening. Software developers are not famed as being the most social of butterflies, everybody ordered the same menu item, strained chit-chat was enjoyed, and we headed back to the hotel for an early night, prior to our morning flight to Spain.

The early morning budget EasyJet flight to Alicante was packed full of already inebriated Glaswegians, excited to be swapping the darkening and sodden winter nights of Scotland for a few sunny days on the beaches and bleary alcohol-fueled nights in the bars of Benidorm. We were heading for the town of Altea, located not far from Alicante which would serve as a base for a few days exploring the local coastal towns. We would then head further south and check out various towns along the Costa Calida, Costa Almeria, and Costa del Sol, before flying back to the United States via Madrid. This trip was of course much more than just sightseeing, by the end of this short week we needed to find, at a minimum, a shortlist of towns we could soon call home.

It was dark when we picked up the rental Mini Cooper in Alicante airport and we immediately got lost in the exit loops of the concourse; it was late and rainy when we arrived at the Hotel. Paula had picked out the Hotel Tossal D'Altea for our first few nights in Spain. It was a wonderful choice. The Hotel is a beautifully restored three-hundred-year-old olive mill just below the Casco Antiguo or Altea Old Town. A free cocktail greets guests, the rooms are clean and expansive, and the beds are comfortable. Everything that can be made of olive oil is for gratis in the guest rooms. A bottle of olive oil is an obvious gift, but the hotel extends its product creativity to the soap, shampoo, conditioner, and even a yellow-tinged toothpaste that strangely lubricated as it cleansed.

We cashed in our free cocktail chits in the form of a couple of beers and then walked in the warm evening drizzle to the beach for dinner. We ate superb Thai food by the Mediterranean Sea and walked back through the Old Town. Out of season in November the town was quiet but remarkably beautiful. Originally Moorish, it was captured and fortified by the Christians in 1244. A maze of steep cobbled streets leads up to the church that stands like a sentinel above the curved bay of the town below. Steps worn by the feet of two hundred generations lead through crooked side streets, each one home to a millennium of lives lived and stories told. Endearing nooks in the ancient fortifications are now home to bars and restaurants, filled with the lights and sounds of Spain. We had an appointment to look at a villa that was for sale further North up the coast in the morning, so after a nightcap at the hotel bar, we collapsed into the massive bed, our first night in Spain complete.

We spent a couple of nights in Altea touring the local countryside and checking out local towns and villages. We ate breathtakingly good steaks and drank homemade Limoncello at Quarara, a restaurant in the old town dominated by views of the electric blue ceramic dome of the church of the Parròquia de Nostra Senyora del Consol. The restaurant was owned by Marco, an outstanding chef from Italy, so friendly and talented that we broke a cardinal travel rule and went back again the next night.

In the nearby 13th-century castle town of Polop, we got almost irrevocably lost when driving up the meandering and rapidly narrowing cobbled streets we were suddenly presented with a sudden dead end and no means of further progression. I had to reverse, stressed and white-knuckled, all the way back down through startled locals. At the bottom of the hill, we found out that Paula had the navigation system set to walk, ah, how I chuckled at the blunder.

We visited Benidorm and ate British fish and chips and drank icy cold Estrella beers in the shade, people-watching as the hordes of partying tourists passed by. Benidorm is one of the few high-rise Spanish coastal towns. It is jammed with bars and clubs and is famed for its free cabaret acts. The British flock to Benidorm, along with Germans, the Belgiums and the Dutch, all there to drink and party in the year-round warm climate and burn, blistering tomato red on the expansive blue flag beaches

But after a few short days, we needed to head South. Our initial feelings regarding Altea were that the town was pleasant and charming but nothing special. The scenery was beautiful for sure, soaring mountains on one side with the crystal shimmering blue of the Mediterranean on the other, with whitewashed villas caught between. But we had itchy feet and believed that the South would have even more to offer.

The next few days sadly proved this was not to be the case. We travelled south along the coast visiting Torrevieja, Los Alcazares, Mazarron, Garucha, and got as far South as Mojacar. Each town had things that offered appeal for sure. The towns of Torrevieja and San Javier hosted large English-speaking communities. Pubs called the Red Lion and The Crown, where you could eat Sunday lunch and watch League Division football proliferated. The houses here were built mostly within large urbanizations, cookie-cutter boxes heaped together along broad roads that whisk tourists from the beaches to the vast shopping malls of Dos Mares and Zenia.

We were excited to see the towns of Los Alcazares, Estrella de Mar, and Los Nietos, towns dotted along the massive Mar Menor. This large coastal saltwater lagoon stretches for fourteen miles along the coast, a narrow sandbar separating it from the Mediterranean. It is seldom more than three feet deep and its warm shallow waters have been a Blue Flag haven for years to both Spanish and foreign tourists due to its beauty, safety, and access to watersport amenities. When we visited it was an ecological disaster. It had become a vast basin that collects the chemical run-offs from the intensively farmed fields to the west. The contamination had been an ongoing problem for years, but the issue was exasperated a month prior to our visit when floods dumped huge amounts of nitrates and other chemicals into the lagoon. It was locally called the 'escándalo de la sopa verde' or green soup scandal, the chemicals turning the once clear blue water a bright oxygen-deprived chemical green, making fish float and paddling toes tingle. We talked to a local estate agent, with offices adjacent to the lagoon, to ask how badly house prices had been impacted by the floods.

"What floods," she replied curtly, "we don't get floods here," this as we watched, mouths agape at the mendacity, council workers replacing emergency sandbags behind her.

Further south still, we ate a wonderful curry at the Sartaj Indian Restaurant in the port town of Mazarron. We stopped at the Hotel La Cumbre situated on the top of a hill that looked out over the sea. It was mostly empty at that time of the season and ridiculously cheap. In Mojacar Playa, we drove along the beautiful coast and marveled at the vast array of bars and restaurants. By dinner time, when we left our hotel to find food they were mostly closed. We finally found a tiny place that still had a light on and we ate fresh sardines, juicy vermillion Garuccha prawns, and Paella, but we were the sole diners. It was delicious, but as we finished eating, the lady owner turned off the lights and stacked chairs. Back in our grimy hotel overlooking the sea, in the fading light, we were startled to see large wild boars, or Jabali, down on the beach, black and tusked, down from the mountains at night to forage on the trash from the tourists.

The towns in the South were largely empty and uninspiring. Out of season for sure, but it was hard to imagine a permanent life here where tourism was the only draw. One of our last days touring the south really made the decision for us. We started the day in high spirits as we planned to visit some of the towns and pueblos we had seen on British TV shows such as 'A Place in the Sun,' and 'Sun, Sea and Selling Houses.' The premise of these shows is that fellow Brits would be shown three properties in the area, and with the help of one of the friendly and knowledgeable British estate agents, quickly and easily find their dream home in the sun.

We drove inland from Mojacar to visit the town of Vera which we knew from the episodes we had watched eagerly back in the US. The church of Parroquia de Nuestra Señora de la Encarnación is the backdrop in the town square, where the initial TV interview with the potential buyer usually takes place. The impression given is of a bustling market town with active bars and shops. In truth, the town is quietly urban, listless, and unremarkable. Uninteresting the day we visited, with the exception of the disproportionate number of young men with broken arms we saw, all taking the air while nursing fresh and drying plaster casts. Hapless apprentices perhaps from a wildly unsuccessful Toreador school? We never found out. I think about it still.

Next on the itinerary was Huercal-Overa, another favorite of these shows. It's actually a large commercial university town located in the dusty gray valley of Alamanzora. Truth be told we didn't give it a chance. We parked the car, gave each other a despondent glance, and drove on.

Our last stop was Tabernas, another 'bustling market town' often vaunted on the popular TV shows as a wonderful place to live. The nearby Tabernas desert was used to shoot many of the famous Spaghetti Westerns of the '70s and '80s. We arrived on a windy and cast-over day to find the town was shut. It was difficult to tell if it had ever really been open. We drove a circuit of the streets, from one end of town to the other, and then reversed course to make sure we hadn't missed some hidden gem. There seemed to be absolutely nothing to recommend the place.

We ate an inhospitable lunch at the only local restaurant we could find. Two locals stopped playing the one-armed bandit to stare at us when we entered, the opening bars to the Good, the Bad, and the Ugly immediately playing unbidden in my head. Once seated in the empty and archaic dining room, the peculiarly coiffured waiter proceeded to list the menu items verbally in Spanish. No written menu at all, just a long list of Spanish words. Paula and I sat with furrowed brows, concentrating and looking at each other as each new item was spoken. When he came to 'Sopa de Pollo' on his mentally regurgitated list, and it being the only item we had understood to this point, we both settled for the chicken soup.

After lunch, we started our route back to Mojacar Beach and our Hotel. In the end, we didn't make it back to the beach resort. We wound our way through dusty roads, any view sheathed and barricaded by seemingly limitless rows of polytunnels. For the area to provide produce year-round, the land around Almeria is now covered in forty-thousand hectares of plastic greenhouses, a veritable Costa del Polythenio. A little depressed by the events and places visited that day, we decided to press on and head back toward Alicante.

We stopped for the night at the Parador Hotel in the ancient Roman city of Lorca. The hotel is built around the towering and imposing ninth-century ruins of the Castillo de Lorca, an impregnable fortress fought over by the Christians and Muslims for nearly eight hundred years, it offered breathtaking views across the darkening valley far below. Out of season, the hotel was mostly empty. A storm developed that evening, the wind whistling eerily around both the hotel and the ancient fortifications. Opened doors would be caught by the wind and slammed shut behind, the boom echoing down the empty hotel corridors that reminded us of a scene from The Shining. We expected to encounter twins in identical petticoat frocks to appear from around a corner of the long corridors and ask us to come play.

In the morning we ate a lonely breakfast of salty sardines, hams, and olives in the vast and mostly vacant dining room before heading to Alicante and our flight to Madrid, and then onward back to Atlanta the following day.

We had a very early dinner on our last night in Madrid at a wonderful steak restaurant, Entrecot de Vacuno with grilled tomatoes so good they may have been sprinkled with crack cocaine. We still talk about them. After eating, as we walked the busy city streets, the nearby offices emptied of workers. It was a Friday, and suddenly the city was crowded, brought to life with surging crowds, street vendors selling beer and tapas, and entertainers singing and playing for Cents and working girls vying for Euros, all amid the striking architecture of the Gran Via. In a nearby bar, drinking post-dinner cocktails we reviewed the trip and while overall it had been mixed, it had mostly been disheartening. Spain has beautiful cities and towns spread across the Mediterranean but move inland only a few miles from the coast and the interior is devastatingly bereft of life.

The one place we both agreed was an option to explore further was Altea. It was both close to airports that could whisk us back to see family in the UK and in reasonable proximity to Benidorm with its large English community. It would at a minimum be a good jumping-off point to explore our new life in Spain.

Ship or Sell

Christmas 2019

As we prepared for our last Christmas in our lovely house in Alpharetta Georgia USA, we had more decisions to make. Did I mention how wonderfully happy we were at that time in that house? We had bought it in 2014 and moved in pretty much to the day, close to Christmas five years prior. We had previously lived only a few miles away in a big old house on a steep hill in Roswell GA. The Roswell house was big and roomy, but dark inside and infrastructurally past its best. We were certain that it was inching its way towards the lip of the hill to inevitably slide itself to destruction.

I was initially reluctant to move, but like all the best decisions in life Paula wanted to move and so we did. We picked a great community of around eighty homes called Westminster in Alpharetta close to bars and restaurants. We completely refurbished the house from top to bottom, purchased the best furniture we had ever hoped to own, designed and built a new saltwater pool, and landscaped the gardens to perfection. Ben was already living in Jacksonville and Adam was sometimes in an apartment with friends or living with us at home depending on circumstances.

We had our three beloved dogs, Tybee our treasured, smart, and loving nine-year-old yellow Labrador who had come to live with us in that first year we moved to the United States. We named her after the island, close to Savannah to which we loved to vacation. Pi came from a rescue, an adorably nervous but cute five-year-old small black mix, with tiny, crooked teeth and a monster underbite, and then Archie, another rescue, he was waiting for me at home when I returned from a business trip to Glasgow. Just three at the time, he had teetered on the edge of existence all his young life, suffering joint issues since he was a puppy. With a curly tail and black muzzle, a vestige of his Pyrenean/Akita cross heritage, he should have looked vicious, but his white socks and ears that never pricked belied his gentle nature. Despite Paula picking him when I was absent, he had claimed me as his own and would, despite his sixty pounds, lie on my lap, legs in the air whimpering for a tummy tickle.

Paula and I had worked hard for everything we had, but we were always thankful that we never lost sight that for two kids from working-class backgrounds in Southport England, we were literally living the best life.

It was against this background that we made the truly hard decision to sell the house in order to fund the next stage of our lives. Our plan was to initially rent for six months to a year in the area around, or preferably in the town of Altea. We discussed with excitement, spending the early days of my newly found retirement jogging to the beach for morning coffee and churros, and the afternoons leisurely searching the nearby towns for a villa we would be happy to purchase.

Throughout those weeks between Thanksgiving and Christmas, we were both active on Idealista, an online Spanish real estate site looking for a suitable rental property. We were looking for a three or four-bedroom villa, preferably with a pool so friends and family could come and visit and spend time with us. A big part of the reason to move back closer to the UK was so we could see more of the family we had left behind when we had moved to the United States. The property search didn't reveal a glut of options. As dog owners come to quickly realize when looking for rental properties anywhere in the world, very few properties want dogs.

The other problem we needed to resolve was what to do with all of our possessions. In early December our initial plan was to take everything with us, ship all our furniture by sea to Barcelona, and have our cars imported into Europe. The dilemma of cost over convenience soon became a reality. If we rented a furnished house, where would we put our possessions? Storage was expensive, particularly as it might be a year before we would be ready to release goods, and importing cars through the bureaucracy of the European Union was going to be costly and complex. Even if we did buy a house in Spain quickly, our furniture was of American taste and proportions and surely certain not to fit either dimensionally or aesthetically into a Spanish villa. Ultimately, we decided to sell everything we had with the exception of the clothes we would need for a balmy Spanish climate, necessary documents, and very few personal items. We would buy everything again when we found our footing and got settled in Spain later in the year.

If we were excited to be nearer to all of the family we had missed in the UK, that Christmas holiday was melancholy, the conclusion of our life in the US.

An end to a wonderful fourteen years of fun and work. We had explored the country, made tremendous friends, eaten ourselves chubby, and played tennis in the sunshine as often as we could. Paula had accumulated a hefty collection of tennis bag tags from victorious matches and I had learned to be a good loser. Every dinner we had with friends felt like a goodbye, every visit to our favorite restaurants and bars, a final farewell. Christmas slowly transitioned to the New Year, the year we would begin another new life. It was thrilling and at the same time terrifying to contemplate.

New Horizons

January 2020

Our expectations in those first days of 2020 were that the year would certainly be a challenge. We understood the difficulties of moving countries, this time to one where the language would be an additional barrier. The plan was coming together though and we were sanguine about the prospects of a successful move.

We had finally found a place on Idealista that looked promising and had started negotiations with Jim and Maria, the owners of the villa just outside Altea. Jim was from Wales in the United Kingdom and his wife was Spanish, although the pair now lived permanently in Belgium. They were happy to take dogs and would even offer up a short-term and flexible lease. We had only seen photos, but with four bedrooms, with a beautiful pool set in mature and colorful gardens, it looked perfect. We spoke to Jim on the phone a few times and he was chatty and affable with a strong accent straight from the Welsh valleys. He was a little scatterbrained, but very flexible around rental terms. His previous tenant had just moved out and the villa was available immediately, but he was OK with us taking up the tenancy mid-year. He actually wanted to get over to Spain in March to do some cleaning and minor repairs prior to our arrival.

We decided on another trip back to Spain, combining it once more with a business meeting with my Glasgow team. I booked international flights for another trip to Glasgow in mid-March. On this trip, both Paula and Adam would accompany me. Adam had decided to leave the US, his home for fourteen of his most formative years, and try life in the UK. We would get him settled with family in our old hometown of Southport and then fly back to Altea to see the villa while Jim was there doing his repairs. If all looked OK, we would sign contracts and plan to move out as early as June or July that same year.

All the component parts of the puzzle were dropping into place beautifully in those early days of January. Our realtor recommended marketing the house in early March to catch the spring market in the USA, with the listing going live on March 13th. With that in mind, we began to sell our belongings in earnest on eBay, Facebook Marketplace, and neighborhood sites. I sold my beloved rally blue Subaru sports car and being American citizens, our guns. Our first and last yard sale was organized for early February.

On the third of January, we completely ignored a low-key news report that was circulating from China. The news item reported forty-four cases of pneumonia in the town of Wuhan, Hubei province. The World Health Organization was paying the event some minor attention as the forty-four initial cases had all unusually been hospitalized and were displaying some curious symptoms, breathing difficulties, and lesions on the lungs. The disease had spread from a local wet market, the Huanan Seafood Wholesale Market.

Similar to farmer's markets, selling fresh fish, meats, and vegetables, these wet markets also sell and slaughter live animals, snakes, beavers, porcupines, and baby crocodiles, among other animals. Viruses spread rapidly if the animals are sick and kept in cramped or dirty conditions. Pathogens intermingle, genetic code mutates, and DNA is swapped between species, and the animal's bodily fluid facilitates the virus jumping to human food handlers and customers. Any virus will spread fastest in areas of dense populations, and in the city of Wuhan, eleven million people lived, crowded together in high-rise urbanizations.

Portents

February 2020

In February, as Boris Johnson casually skipped five National Cabinet Office Briefings (colloquially known as COBRA), relating to the new COVID-19 breakout that had assiduously and silently spread from China to at least six other countries, cases in the UK reached double digits. In the US where Patricia Dowd a 57-year-old resident of California became the first COVID-19 death in the United States, Donald Trump famously quipped, "The coronavirus is very much under control in the USA...Stock Market starting to look very good to me!"

At least initially, the new Severe Acute Respiratory Syndrome Coronavirus 2 (SARS-CoV-2) appeared to be just another virus from Asia of the same ilk as the SARS-CoV-1 outbreak of 2002-2004. That outbreak claimed the lives of 774 people worldwide, but not a single case in the USA and only four non-lethal cases in the UK. Or perhaps that of Ebola in 2014 that claimed 11,000 lives worldwide, but in the US, only a single life. Troubling and scary for sure, but developed nations with prepared governments, mature technology, and highly functioning healthcare systems had historically proven they could control and contain such diseases and mitigate their effects.

No precautions were being taken in the USA at that time. Bars and businesses were open as normal and nobody wore a mask or carried hand sanitizer. The focus was on bringing US Citizens home from viral hotspots around the globe, particularly from the Diamond Princess cruise ship.

It really wasn't on anybody's radar in those first few weeks of February. We had folks turning up at our house on a regular basis to buy furniture and other household items, shaking hands and exchanging cash. We even had our frigid yard sale on the 22nd of February. It was brutally cold for the first few hours, at least until the sun broke cover of the trees, and sales were slow. Nobody showed up with a mask and the general mood about the virus was an overwhelming lack of interest. It was something happening to other countries and, if we mentioned Spain when asked why we were selling so much stuff, we generally received mutters of concern and confusion as to why we would risk traveling to such a third-world place.

Of course, the virus was present in the United States and spreading just as quickly as it was in Europe. Just nobody in government wanted to admit it. At a press conference on February 26th Trump stated clearly, or as clearly as he was capable,

"When you have fifteen people, and the fifteen within a couple of days is going to be down close to zero, that's a pretty good job we've done".

Pandemic

March 2020

Our first real inkling that the situation was worsening was on a quick visit to our local Publix supermarket. Unknown to us folks with grown kids, Fulton County had earlier announced the closing of the schools after a single government employee had been diagnosed with the disease. It was March 9th, and the supermarket was a complete warzone, the checkouts jammed with trolleys stacked high with pasta, booze, and toilet rolls. The shelves were already emptying. We did some panic buying of our own (we were already there after all), mainly in the form of boxes of red wine and spam. We were such fools; toilet roll didn't even occur to us!

We still didn't really worry that the epidemic would adversely impact our overall plan to move, although we prudently decided to cancel our plan to visit the UK and Spain after the World Health Organization declared a global pandemic on March 11th. We looked again at the photos we had received of the villa in Spain and made the decision to just go ahead and contract to rent the place sight unseen. The monthly rent was reassuringly expensive, and the location and pictures represented it well. Our initial contract would only be for three months—honestly, how bad could it be?

The US banned the arrival of non-US citizens from Europe on Friday, March 13th and Spain went into local lockdown the following day. That was the week we would have been in Spain, so we breathed a huge sigh of relief that we had canceled the trip. We found out soon after that Jim, the owner of the villa, had just arrived in Spain to clean and prepare the villa for our arrival. He would be locked down there, unable to leave and away from his family for the foreseeable future.

The thirteenth and fourteenth of March were a busy few days for the world and us in particular. Knowing we were leaving the US Healthcare system; I had been maximizing my company's healthcare benefits. I had been to the doctors and been awarded a diagnosis of hypertension, the dentists to enjoy a crown, and even been to the dermatologist's office to receive the all-clear. The morning of the thirteenth was both the date we put the house on the market and the date of my first colonoscopy.

The day prior I hadn't been able to stray more than a fifteen-second sprint from the bathroom, don't ask how I knew the precise figure. Thankfully, earlier in the year, we had quite literally splashed out on a luxury bidet toilet that warmed the seat and soothed and freshened any sore parts with a jet of warm water. With viewings in the afternoon, and Paula otherwise preoccupied with preparing the house, Adam drove me to the hospital. The procedure, as most folks who have finally plucked up the courage to do so realize, was uneventful, but the medication left me woozy and confused and Adam wildly amused at my wobbliness and rambling mutterings.

We had multiple viewings that afternoon while I was still recovering from the combined effects of the ordeal and anesthetic, so to my surprise, we were under contract the following morning. We agreed on a closing date of May 6th, a huge fifty-six days distant, which we figured would give us plenty of time to sell the remainder of our belongings and for this pesky darn global pandemic to all just blow over.

In those naïve days of mid to late March, our plans went back and forth as we juggled the variables. A family joke, we laughed, comparing it to the riddle of the fox, the hen, and the grain. In this old riddle, the farmer must cross the river in his little boat getting all three to the far bank, all safe and sound. But he can only take one item at a time. If he takes the fox, the hen will eat the grain. If he takes the grain, the fox will eat the hen. The solution is both simple and complex at the same time, a play on logic and logistics. We foolishly prided ourselves at that time on having a plan so cunning even that wily fox would be impressed.

By the morning of the closing on May 6th, we would have the house empty, except for the two suitcases we had allowed each other for the move. We would drive to the solicitor's office in Paula's Honda Pilot. On the way home to pick up the cases, we would sell the Honda to CarMax, the local car supermarket. Then we just needed to get the dogs on their way to the airport and Uber ourselves there shortly afterward for our flight to Barcelona and subsequent drive down the coast to Altea and our new life. Since Adam's trip to the UK to start his new life there had been canceled, he decided to initially accompany us to Spain and move back to the UK when life settled to some semblance of normality across Europe.

Regarding the virus, the United States at that time was a cocoon of ignorance and avoidance. Restrictions were almost non-existent, and precautions were becoming a political axe. We had no bathroom tissue, but of course, we had a bidet toilet. The bars had closed but all the restaurants were offering curbside. Nobody wore a mask or carried hand sanitizer and most shops and businesses traded as normal. The White House continued to play down the serious nature of the disease, offering misleading and obfuscating statements. Trump again offered,

"The virus is very much under control," as the number of cases in the US leaped from the hundreds in early March to close to a truly startling two hundred thousand by the end of the month.

Living in the cocoon we didn't immediately realize how badly the situation was worsening globally, with Spain taking the brunt of the infections in Europe. An aging population closely packed together in hotspots such as Madrid and Barcelona, coupled with insufficient hospital capacity, the disease had led to a surge in deaths sixty-eight percent higher than the annual average. The Spanish government declared an initial fifteen-day state of alarm on the 13th of March but then extended it until April 12th after cases continued to rise. Airlines were starting to be restricted by rapidly changing government mandates. The situation was further complicated by the dogs and their flights. Atlanta is hot most of the year and simply scorching in the middle of summer, so the airlines have moratoriums on livestock travel during the hottest months of July and August. If we couldn't get them out before the end of June, we would be stuck here until Fall. Our cunning plan was starting to look startlingly over-optimistic, and it looked like we would need a place to stay here in the United States well beyond the date in May when our house would be sold and we had banked on flying out to Barcelona.

Shady Grove

April 2020

We began a search for rental properties and alternative means of transport for the dogs. We quickly found out that no rentals would accept more than two dogs, we looked at corporate short-term rentals and even Hotels and Airbnb's. Our timing was horrendous. Airbnb properties in the area that had been available prior to the arrival of the virus were now being used by their actual owners to provide bolt holes, places to stock up, and lockdown.

We finally contracted on a run-down, but really well-located property only a few miles away, in Shady Grove Lane in downtown Alpharetta. A friend had recommended talking to her nephew who was starting out as a realtor, and he found a small ranch house that had been purchased by the owner for demolition and subsequent re-development. The subdivision was old but well cared for and within walking distance of the popular downtown. The streets were lined by big old ranch houses on large tree-filled lots, the type at risk of going extinct in Atlanta as they get replaced by large, million-dollar family homes.

The limited lockdown in Atlanta had meant building permits had been delayed, and the owner was happy for us to rent it to us on a somewhat flexible basis for the next few months. The fact that it had been bought for demolition wouldn't normally find its way into a realtor's listing, and the house was indeed dated, but it was surprisingly habitable and with the exception of the horror film-themed basement, reasonably insect-free.

We slowed down the sale of our few remaining essential items such as beds, sofas, and TVs so we would have the basics available in the unfurnished house. I rented a big old U-Haul truck from a nearby Home Depot and with the help of

Adam and Mike, our wonderful and endlessly good mood-spreading neighbor we moved out on the last day of April.

The next day, with skinned knuckles and aching muscles inflicted by the move, I climbed into the attic space and began to spray insecticide to kill the few roaches I expected to find in such an old house. As the first jet hit the scant insulation and cobweb-coated eaves, a scene redolent of arachnophobia, but with ten thousand cockroaches replacing the role of the killer spiders began to play out before my eyes. The thriving horror emerged en masse from their dark and secretive lairs. They scurried everywhere as they panicked, as did I in turn, when I saw the horde swarm towards me from their dank hiding places. In my revulsion, I hopped and danced and made quiet squeaky noises of grunted dismay as they crawled over my shoes, wishing I had worn long pants tucked stiffly into thick socks instead of the sports trainers and shorts I had on. I tried not to fall through the ceiling, still squirting insecticide recklessly in all directions, as they continued to scamper and writhe towards me, desperate to escape the spray.

I did the same thing later in the basement, now with nerves jangling and a nervous tick to boot, furiously brushing falling dust and grime from head and shoulders, certain that the swarming, squirming horde had followed me from the attic and were intent upon overwhelming me and penetrating every unprotected orifice, ear holes, nose holes, and other holes, to burrow with malign intent towards the brain and other sensitive organs, to turn me slowly but inexorably into a shambling effigy of Edgar the bug man from Men in Black.

Job done I walked back upstairs on unsteady legs, hands trembling and considering that I would, perhaps, need a less active imagination if I was to ever enter permanent employment in the extermination business.

The next day I tidied and mowed the unkempt yard, Paula and Adam painted the inside walls, and we bought some multi-colored pansies from Home Depot and planted them in the window boxes. It began to resemble a home again. Neat and tidy as its neighbors for a while. We felt we had given the house, and ourselves, a brief respite from the next part of our respective journeys. We bought an inflatable above-ground pool for the deck and we prepared to hunker down for what we assumed would be the remainder of the summer and early fall.

A Window of Opportunity

May 2020

On the evening of May 5th, we said final goodbyes to our lovely old house with drinks around the pool with friends and neighbors. The evening was Atlanta warm, heady with the scent of Jessamine, too early in the year for fireflies but loud with the chattering crepitation of cicadas. We ordered pizza and wings and with the house empty, and all our furniture already moved to Shady Grove, we sat around the brightly lit pool on wobbly camp stools and chatted and laughed. In the morning, we closed at the solicitor's office and drove back to Shady Grove in a conflicted mood. We were simultaneously relieved that the sale had gone through at a good market price but saddened and frustrated that we were unable to get to Spain and start our new life.

The international travel situation had not improved, and most international flights were now canceled. Europe had taken the pandemic with the utmost seriousness and had shut down, businesses closed, and citizens confined to their homes. Countries were still shuttered to visitors and struggling to control infection rates. Jim, the Welsh owner of the villa we had rented was still in lockdown in Spain, his wife and son locked down separately in Belgium. We called Jim to check on him and jokingly reminded him that he really had no excuse now to not have the villa sparkling when we finally arrived. He was clearly bored and tired of his own company; it took Paula twenty minutes to get him off the phone.

I checked the travel news three or four times a day. Spain had just announced de-escalation plans that would run for several weeks, with a final lift on restrictions aiming for the first week of July, almost certainly too late for us to get the dogs transported out of Atlanta.

This raised a growing concern that had been in the back of our minds since our plans to leave the US first formed. Our lovely Labrador Tybee was now thirteen and was not doing well. She had recovered from cancer a few years back and then suffered a couple of serious bouts of pancreatitis, we had said our goodbyes to her yellow loveliness several times. She was however incredibly resilient and bounced back each time. One aspect that was more concerning was that she had become terribly anxious and would shake uncontrollably and cower from us at the slightest noise. We often found ourselves tiptoeing around the kitchen carefully placing plates and pans so as not to disturb her. It became such a habit that I still find myself doing it. It seemed unlikely she would survive an international flight in the hold of an aircraft.

We looked at every alternative including transporting the pets across the Atlantic on the Queen Mary. The Queen Mary sails from New York to Portsmouth and is the only ship of its kind to also transport the passenger's pets. The animal berths were booked solid for the next three years – honestly, what sort of person knows they are going to need a transatlantic berth for Mr. Tiddles three years in advance? We even looked into freighters that would take passengers, but their sailing times between the US and Europe were in the order of months. It was an issue we would need to resolve but at that moment there was nothing we could really plan for.

Like most of the world in early May we were in an enforced hiatus. We spent our days walking Pi and Archie around the local streets and parks, Tybee now being too old to make the distance. We made some more improvements to the rental house even though we knew it would soon be demolished. In the back we strung lights across the deck, it all really made a difference to the place. We had nothing to do but sit and wait. Paula had come to the conclusion that nothing was changing before the onset of summer and had resolved herself to spend the next few months in Shady Grove.

The time was used to double down on learning Spanish. We had both been using Duolingo, an app-based learning platform that leverages different modes of learning, listening, reading, writing, and speaking in different combinations. Leagues and games keep students engaged and it was pretty fun and helpful. Duo himself is a little green animated owl that pops up to add encouragement during lessons, and if you've been absent for a day or two, an email threatening vague retribution.

It was the morning of Friday 22nd May when we got a surprise email from the dog shipping company. There was a rumor that limited international routes were about to open up a little. Nothing could be confirmed until the following week, but it seemed that British Airways would operate a restricted service for freight and animals only, beginning in June and only to London Heathrow. Were we interested?

As British Airways was only open to shipping freight and livestock, we had to find an alternative service for ourselves. I spent four hours trying to get through to Delta on the platinum member hotline. When I finally spoke to an agent, she confirmed we could get a flight for Paula, Adam, and myself on the evening of June 17th from Atlanta directly to Heathrow. It wasn't Spain but it was Europe and at that point, it seemed close enough.

On the following Friday, we made the decision. We would all fly to London and leave the United States. We would plan to stay for a few short days with Paula's sister Karen in the small village of Tetsworth. Karen is one of the four sisters, Paula being the youngest separated by Karen in age by Lynne, and the eldest sister, Janice. Karen, or Kaz to those who know her well is the easiest of the four, my own dear wife included, the least likely to say a harsh word or sour a friendship. She is married to Steve, a successful TV and film editor. Their house is small but charming, with a large garden, located in the tiny village of Tetsworth just twelve miles from Oxford. It would be a challenge even for a few days in their house, with a total of five adults and four dogs, but for only a day or two, we would make it work. While we were there, I would somehow find us a car to purchase and we would drive across France and Spain to the villa, to hopefully arrive in time for the final de-escalation phase of the Spanish state of alarm. I called British Airways and Delta and made the reservations. We would all be leaving the US on Wednesday, June 17th.

A Farewell

June 13th, 2020

To readers of gentler dispositions and anybody who love companions of a fluffier nature, I warn you now, this will be a short chapter, and not at all at one with the gentle whimsy I have tried hard to convey in the rest of the book.

Early on the morning of the 13th of June, we woke to a crashing, thrashing noise in the bedroom. Tybee had suffered a *massive* stroke and had managed to get herself stuck, half under a floor-standing dressing room mirror. She was conscious but terribly distressed and confused and, for the first time ever, had soiled herself. My dear old girl, was unable to stand so I carried her, tears streaming down my face in dismay, into the yard to pee.

It was absolutely heartbreaking to see her this way. We made her as comfortable as we could back in the house, but we figured, based on her lack of awareness, that today might be her last and we would need to have her put to sleep. By the afternoon, however, she appeared a little better, so we carried her into the yard to relieve herself and then put her to bed. But in the morning, she was no brighter, she had limited control of her limbs and would stagger and fall heavily if we weren't constantly there to help her.

Our eldest son Ben came up from the naval base in Jacksonville to visit and say his farewells. Tybee's condition was not improving, and we had a terrible decision to make.

On the morning of the 15th, a Monday, sunny and hot under a clear cerulean Atlanta sky we were all waiting on the deck outside Shady Grove. We had arranged for the vet to come to the house and put our gorgeous, lovely, beautiful, darling, big old girl to sleep.

Tybee had defined, bracketed, our time in America. She had joined our family as a chunky, floppy puppy in the first few months we had arrived in America. She had helped all of us, in a myriad of ways to settle into our new lives. She had both wagged farewell and later enthusiastically greeted the boys when the school bus came, marking the beginning and end of those awkward first days. She had been the tummy I had rubbed to calm myself when work in this new country had proved just too strange and stressful. She had jogged around the wooded trails opposite the house with Paula on both hot and humid and cold and frigid days. She had been a stalwart companion and the best of friends to us all.

We had adored her. And now like the taught spring of a grandfather clock wound to match the life span of its owner, it had slowly ticktocked itself towards finality. It seemed that our departure from America had somehow become entwined with that spring, synchronized with her last moments, our time here, so sweetly shared, had come to a bitter departure, a terrible farewell.

We arranged her comfortably on her familiar memory foam bed, outside, on the deck. Pi and Archie sniffed inquisitively and the rest of us, uniquely, tragically really, were all together as a family for once, knelt or sat around her while the vet administered the drugs.

She gently closed eyes the color of marmalade, let ginger eyelashes fold to seal perennially closed on cheeks, once yellow but now greyed by age, and she slipped slowly away from us, as eight tender loving hands hugged her body and stroked her face while we individually cried and whispered our shuddering goodbyes.

Leaving the USA

June 17th, 2020

With the deadline for travel at our heels, we shifted back into selling mode. All the furniture and household goods we had moved to Shady Grove all needed to be sold or gifted. We made several trips to local charity outlets, although even they were starting to shut their doors at that point of the epidemic in America. We still had two cars to sell so we took Adam's Toyota RAV4 to CarMax and cashed that out. Now we only had Paula's Honda to take care of on the morning of our planned departure. We started a fresh and final round of saying goodbye to people and places. The tangible difference was that we now had a real deadline with booked and confirmed airline tickets. Paula organized all the complex necessities of veterinarian jabs and certificates to get animals through customs and into Europe, finalized details with the pet shipping company and we were set to go.

The COVID-19 infection rate had peaked in the UK during the first week of May. The strict 'stay at home' order enforced by the UK Government on the 23rd of March had worked and had materially reduced infection rates and new cases. That being said, only nine days before our flight, Boris Johnson decided to introduce a seemingly random, but mandatory, fourteen-day quarantine for new travelers arriving into the UK. The European Union joined us in our outrage and criticism. If the UK was going to impose travel restrictions, it should have done so much earlier in the outbreak. It made no sense to anybody to do so at this late juncture. Germany and Italy were at that time all loosening their restrictions relating to cross-border travel. Either way, we were committed to travel. We had no choice to impose on Kaz and Steve and their small house for the fourteen-day period until we would be free to set off again for Spain.

The night before our flight, the three of us had takeaway food drank red wine sat on the floor of the sparse rental. We would sleep on our mattress which was on the floor of the bedroom, the bedframe having been sold days prior. The mattress was being picked up for trash in the morning. We woke early. Our old neighbor and friend Bob popped around and picked up the last few items and promised to pick us up from CarMax around noon after we had sold Paula's Honda and drop us back at the rental in time for the dogs to be picked up by the pet carrier company mid-afternoon. Bob would swing by again and transport us to the international terminal for our evening flight. It was a crazy busy day. We should have been sad, excited, nervous but we were numbed by the enormity of what we were doing, overwhelmed by the act now set in progress.

We were both more worried about the dogs than anything else. Archie is a terrible traveler, car sick from when Paula picked him up from the pound to this day. Both Archie and Pi had been given light breakfasts and a good walk and there was nothing more we could do. It was with some significant relief when they were safely picked up and headed for the airport. Out of our hands now, all we could do was hope to see them both well when they got delivered to Paula's sister's house in England the following day.

With the dogs on their way to the airport, the three of us spent the rest of the afternoon packing and re-packing suitcases. We had finally managed to get our worldly possessions into two large suitcases each and some small carry-on bags.

All of our worldly possessions

At last, we were set to go. Bob picked us up early for the drive to Hartsfield Jackson International terminal. We needed to avoid the curfews that were active in Atlanta at that time. George Floyd had been killed by police in Minneapolis on May 25th sparking protests nationwide. The situation was further aggravated by the subsequent police killing of Rayshard Brooks outside a Wendy's restaurant here in Atlanta only five nights ago. These awful events had led to Black Lives Matter protests across Atlanta and its environs, prompting the Governor of Georgia, Brian Kemp, to announce a state of emergency. The National Guard had been mobilized and nightly protests had seen tensions escalate between police and protesters.

With the combination of the virus and the curfews, there was little traffic on the normally crowded interstate, and we arrived early at the International Terminal. We unloaded the truck and said our final goodbyes to Bob. It was a genuinely sad and poignant moment as we watched him drive away. Now we three were all on our own and about to leave the USA, the place we had made a home for fourteen years. All of our belongings were sadly stowed in a bunch of bulging suitcases. If there was a note of remorse or doubt at that point, standing curbside watching Bob's truck disappear, it was far too late to action. The decision had been made, the dam holding back the river of events that would lead us to Spain removed, the river was running, and all we could do now was follow the fast-flowing current to where it led.

Inside, the concourse was desolate, a cold and echoing chamber. Air travel was decimated by the pandemic. Once the busiest airport in the world, it was now bereft of the thousands of business and holiday travelers who previously teemed and jostled through check-in and security to reach the duty-free shops and restaurants that supplied the international gates. The security line had been moved to what looked like a teenager's basement, a handful of scruffy TSA agents milled around with little to occupy them. Adam, as always happens, got pulled out of line and frisked by one of the agents. He always leaves something forbidden by the airline in his bag, like it's his first time flying, a nail file maybe, some lithium batteries, or half a pound of marijuana. Whatever it was they seemed satisfied, and just as I was walking back to bail him out, they let him through.

Walking Dead had been filmed in Atlanta, and now with all businesses shuttered, only a few forlorn travelers such as ourselves remained to shuffle mournfully, zombie like through the now silent soulless expanse. It was against this backdrop of a country, being both torn in two through social unrest, and now leading the world in total COVID-19 cases and deaths, that we waited at the gate for our flight to depart.

An English Quarantine

June 18th to July 1st, 2020

Arrivals and customs at Heathrow Airport mirrored the mood in Atlanta. The flight was a third full, with empty seats being used to physically separate travelers, so the usually long line at customs was short. Passenger locator forms needed to be completed to allow authorities to track and trace new arrivals into the country in the case of an outbreak. These were dutifully collected by disinterested customs officers. As in Atlanta, all the shops, bars, and duty-free outlets were closed and the now vast, empty vacuum of the airport weighed heavily on us few stragglers who hauled their baggage into the arrival hall.

We were picked up by the car we had pre-arranged and arrived at Paula's sister's house an hour or so later. The dogs arrived later that day, delivered from Heathrow by the pet courier company, both in surprisingly good condition, happy, wagging, and pleased to see us, and we, them. With bags unloaded and dogs fed, watered, and cuddled, we all settled in for the fourteen-day quarantine period. The UK quarantine rules were both stringent and open to interpretation. New arrivals to the country had to proceed directly to the location where they were planning to self-isolate. That is unless the journey was long, in which case an overnight stay was permitted. Travel by public transport was prohibited unless it was necessary, in which case it was allowed. Once at the location you planned to self-isolate you could not leave that location for the fourteen-day period. Unless groceries, medicine, or the services of a doctor, vet, or lawyer were needed.

We found England's approach to the virus to be a contradiction in many ways. As a population, the British follow rules well, particularly when compared to what we had witnessed in the United States. There were many adherents to the restrictions who had not seen loved ones since March, literally not having left their home since the lockdown was imposed, not going out for groceries or exercise, not even walking their dogs. And yet the news was also full of images of crowded beaches and illegal gatherings in town centers. Despite the incongruencies of the government's approach, it was at least understandable in light of the need to both contain the virus and attempt to keep the economy ticking over. Europe and most of the rest of the world had followed similar protocols. It was a startling contrast to what we had experienced in the USA.

The weather was exceptional for England, a true heatwave. It was certainly no hardship being quarantined. We drank beer, sunbathed in the garden, had bacon sandwiches for lunch, and roasted lamb for dinner. We purchased a huge eight-person tent, partly in readiness for the journey across France and Spain, but mainly to torment and test the patience of Kaz's increasingly long-suffering husband Steve. Me and Adam practiced putting it up in the garden, sweating and trying to decipher the Japanese Kanji and stick-figure instructions, while everybody else shouted helpfully Prosecco-fueled instructions from the shade of the garden bench. We had visions of turning up at a well-provisioned campsite in the Dordogne after a hard day driving, popping up the tent while sipping a nice Bordeaux, slipping into a deep sleep, and waking refreshed and ready for the onward journey.

We decided it would be prudent to do a test camp. Paula and I spent a troubled night without sleep. If you want to sleep on the hard ground, but not immediately, an inflatable mattress is a perfect solution. It was sweltering, unpleasant, and uncomfortable, the inflatable mattress deflated slowly but deliberately through the night, dumped us inexorably and inelegantly, limbs akimbo onto the damp groundsheet. In the morning we began to research the availability of Airbnb's.

We spent the days in confinement watching TV or sitting, chatting in the sunny garden. We each took a turn on the treadmill, running for an hour, more to make the hour pass and gain some solitude than attain some fitness goal. Each week the local supermarket delivered fresh essential produce to us in our exile, more bacon, lamb, and beers. We passed the time in good company, and if the close proximity became too much for some reason, one or more of us would quietly take ourselves to a bedroom, and doze or read a book in amiable silence for a while. The fourteen days were slipping by and we needed to start considering the onward journey.

The good news was that Europe was starting to emerge from the lockdown period. The French land border with Spain, closed since March had re-opened on June 21st, and a route from the UK into France using the channel tunnel would open on July 1st. We began to prepare for the next stage of the journey, and we needed a car large enough to transport three adults, two dogs, and all of our belongings across Europe. I found what looked to be ideal at a nearby second-hand car dealer, a thirteen-year-old Blue Ford Mondeo Estate car, a Dagenham dustbin as one friend noted, in reference to its place of manufacture and predilection to rust. Even better, it appeared that fortune had smiled upon us, it was Left-hand Drive and still registered in Spain. I bought it sight unseen, the only way to do business in a pandemic, and arranged to pick it up on Adam's birthday.

We celebrated Adam's twenty-fifth birthday on June 30th with bottles of Prosecco, a cheap cake bought from a newsagent's shop, and an escape from quarantine. We joyfully walked the dogs across the local fields, leaving the house for the first time in fourteen days. Later in the afternoon, Steve dropped me at the car dealership, run by two friendly Asian lads selling secondhand motors from a seedy lockup outside London. The Mondeo was filthy inside, but it started just fine and ran well on the drive back to the house. The left-hand drive steering wheel made driving awkward on British roads, made more difficult by my not having driven in the UK for a number of years. We spent the rest of the day cleaning the car and doing some test packing.

The plan now was to get the car serviced somewhere locally and then leave Kaz and Steve's house early on the morning of July 2nd and head to Folkestone. We would use the Channel Tunnel to make the zippy thirty-five-minute crossing to Calais and then drive through Paris to our first stop south of the city.

Escape

July 2nd, 2020

July 2nd, the day of departure came around quickly. The car had been serviced the previous day and it came back with a solid prognosis from the friendly and chatty mechanic. He had driven old bangers across Europe in his misguided youth and optimistically gave us an almost fifty-fifty chance of getting there. As we settled the bill, he casually mentioned that the air conditioning wasn't functional, and he hadn't been able to repair it. No big deal in the United Kingdom, where summer temperatures seldom soar into the low seventies, easily solved by opening a window or two, but we were bound for far, far sunnier climbs. With our train to France booked for the following day, it seemed that there was simply no time to look at alternatives or seek repairs elsewhere. This would be a decision we would regret.

That morning, the car was packed. Not an inch of space existed. We had emptied the hard travel cases we had brought from America and bundled clothing into vacuum bags to conserve and optimize space. The dogs and Adam were on the back seats with everything else we owned jammed and crammed into whatever nook or cranny remained. At six am we said our goodbyes to Kaz and Steve. Kaz was tearful, emotional to see us go, and already making plans to come and visit the villa in September. Steve's emotions ran deeper and were hard to decipher, but he seemed grateful for the shed full of abandoned travel cases, the tent, and the fifteen-foot square of dying grass it had left behind. We will be eternally grateful to them for sharing their home with us for our quarantine, but after the fourteen days of containment, we were ready to hit the road and restart our journey to Spain and the Villa in Altea.

There was a startling amount of traffic, given the country was technically still in lockdown as we navigated around the M25 which encircles London, but we made good progress and arrived in time to catch an earlier train across the English Channel. The Channel Tunnel, colloquially known as the 'Chunnel' in the UK, had been completed in 1994, but this would be the first time we had used it to cross the Channel. The idea of a tunnel below the English Channel connecting England to France had been proposed as far back as 1802. This early proposal would use oil lamps to light the way and an artificial island halfway across to allow the coachmen to change horses. Thankfully, that proposal died with Albert Mathieu-Favier, the French engineer who proposed it.

The existing tunnel is the longest underwater section of any tunnel in the world, comprising two active tunnels and a service tunnel running a total distance of thirty-one miles and being a scary three-hundred and eighty feet below sea level at its deepest point. On previous trips to Europe, we had used the old ferry crossings which could take ninety minutes, with lengthy loading and unloading procedures added to that. The channel tunnel crossing would allow us to get to France in a quarter of that time.

Trucks carrying freight to and from the UK had been classed as an essential business and had continued to use the tunnel throughout the lockdowns across Europe. Still, the terminal was quiet, having only re-opened for normal passenger traffic the day prior. Passenger volume in a normal year was typically twenty million people a year but that morning the terminal was mostly deserted, a handful of business travelers and others like us, attempting to cross Europe to return to homes in France, Germany, and Spain. The terminal building which usually housed restaurants and food outlets was mostly closed with only toilet access permitted.

We passed through customs and drove onto the lower deck of the train. A steward ensures the cars are parked closely together, and then individual compartments of the train are claustrophobically closed and secured. With creaks and squeals, the train jerked into motion and picked up speed. Within moments we were underground and below the English Channel, being whisked toward the continent. Ears popped at the lowest point underwater and fifteen minutes later the sensation of deceleration was accompanied by morning sunlight as a French dawn flooded the compartment. We had made it out of England, one step closer to our final destination.

We disembarked in Calais amid a clutter of industrial warehouses and transportation buildings. There were few vehicles on the Autoroute de Anglais, mostly trucks heading toward Paris. Normally the roads just South of Calais would be full of British cars, drivers nervous during the first few miles driving on the right, passengers excited to be heading to the beaches of the South, or campsites in Brittany or the Dordogne. Unusually, we were almost exclusively the only foreign car heading South. Our goal was an Airbnb that Paula had booked in the small town of Saran, just North of Orleans. The remainder of the drive would be around five hours and would take us through Paris.

Unlike the roads to the North, Paris was typically choked with cars, trucks, and motorcycles. It is said that all roads lead to Rome, which is certainly the case in Italy, but in France, all roads lead through Paris, and the road used to circumnavigate Paris is the Boulevard Peripherique. The Construction of the Boulevard Peripherique began in 1958 and was completed in 1973. It is unique in that it was built over the remains of the Thiers Wall, an ancient defensive fortification that once encircled the city. Due to this design, the entrance and exits from the Peripherique coincide with the location of the ancient city gates, or portes of the city. The road is also unusually and remarkably close to the city center, it is only a twenty-two-mile drive around the entire circumference. Compare that to the I-285 which takes sixty-four miles to circumnavigate Atlanta or the M25, the one-hundred and seventeen-mile stretch of ring road around London. It is so close that the Eiffel Tower itself can often be glimpsed between the buildings that buttress up against the highway. It has become a permanent gridlock for travelers, and the heavy urban sprawl of modern Paris has completely encompassed it, limiting its ability to add capacity by expanding outward.

On a typical day, the Peripherique will transport a quarter of a million vehicles around the city center. By late afternoon when we arrived, they were all there waiting for us. We crawled slowly westbound, in formation with the other cars and trucks while maniacal motorcycles screamed past, indignant at our presence on the narrow two lanes. We wound the windows down to get some air flowing through the hot car, but the traffic noise that reverberated from the tunnel walls was horrendous and upset both Archie and Pi more than the heat. At one point, Google Maps took us off the Peripherique and onto some back roads only to immediately recalculate and tell us that we should be back on the road it just took us off. I was forced to accelerate across three crowded lanes of hostile traffic, and possibly a red traffic light or two to get back on the Peripherique at the next junction, eliciting Adam to comment that he was, "NEVER going to drive in Europe".

But slowly we made progress and eventually, we found our exit at the Porte de Gentilly and then onto the Autoroute de Soleil, the main autoroute that whisks tourists to the Mediterranean towns of the south of France. Congestion immediately started to ease and then tailed off further as we exited onto the A10 or L'Aquitaine toward Bordeaux. Ninety minutes later we pulled into Saran and parked the hot, engine-popping Mondeo outside the Airbnb. We were met by the owner who lived next door.

I had studied French for three years when at school in the UK and had visited France a few times through the years. But now, years later, and confronted by a real Frenchman, I couldn't understand a single word and my memory of even basic French failed me completely. We gesticulated at each other for a few minutes and between Paula and myself, we think we figured out that he wanted to know when we would depart in the morning, and where we should drop the key when we did. He handed this to us and quickly ran back to his house to avoid further complicated conversations.

The house was really lovely, a welcome haven after our first day on the road. It was typically Gallic in both design and decoration, but clean and well-provisioned. We had brought food and drinks from the UK, so after walking the dogs around a nearby lake we cracked open some cold beers and settled in to watch the incomprehensible French TV shows. We were all extremely fatigued. That day we had covered nearly four hundred miles and including the channel tunnel train crossing, we had been on the road for over nine hours. But we had Paris behind us and better roads ahead and we were another day closer to our Mediterranean dream.

Archie and Pi at the end of a long day

An Evening with Henry

July 3rd, 2020

The next day we woke late and had breakfast. Our destination was Castets only five or six hours away, so we had some time to prepare for the day. We walked the dogs around the lake close to the house, re-packed the car, dropped the key in the lockbox we think the owner had indicated the previous day, and hit the road. The town of Castets is situated in Southwestern France close to the Atlantic Ocean and just north of the Pyrenees. It would be our last stop in France before crossing the Pyrenees themselves and entering Spain.

The journey was pleasingly uneventful. The toll roads were well maintained, and we made fast easy progress. It was hot in the car with no air conditioning but whenever traffic slowed, we cranked the windows down to refresh the air. The big old diesel engine of the Mondeo pulled us along fast and easy, south past the towns of Tours, Poitiers, and Saintes.

We pulled off the autoroute and into a service station to fill the car with diesel. With the car topped off, we parked up in the heat and took a moment to stretch. This was Adam's first time in France, and he had a dream of sipping an espresso, so he optimistically headed inside with his non-existent French to try and procure one. The service station was busy with travelers, we had no idea where everybody was going given the country had only recently emerged from a lockdown. Inside the service station, everybody was wearing a mask, and hand sanitizer was made available at the entrance. We bought baguettes from the well-stocked and varied delicatessen. We found some grass in the rear of the parking area and let the dogs walk around and cool down. There was some seating in the shade, and the dogs happily and nosily drank cold water while we ate our sandwiches, crammed with cheese and salami, French saucisson, salty and delicious.

Back on the road, we were now driving through the Bordeaux vineyards, heavy with purple ripening fruit, parallel lines of vines that stretched mile upon mile across the undulating hills, dotted with the occasional spire of a distant chateau. Dense groves of poplar trees cast long shadows on the hills as we continued south and then, without warning we were across the Dordogne River which empties from the Massif Central into the Atlantic twenty miles west. Traffic slowed as we approached the world heritage city of Bordeaux itself.

It was hot in the car, but the slower traffic allowed us to, once again, crack the windows and freshen the air. This close to the ocean the air had the tang of the seaside and carried the sound of gulls. Archie and Pi perked up in the back sensing our proximity to the sea and perhaps anticipating the end of the day's journey. We snaked slowly through the industrial environs of the city. The Garonne River was in the distance, broad and unhurried, the color of this morning's coffee. We crossed on the Pont d'Aquitaine, and then the last long hour onward to Castets itself. That last hour was wearisome for everybody, the landscape flat and monotonous, the ripe hills had given way to salty sea marshes. We were all stiff, sweaty, and cramped, but traffic was thankfully light and our destination for the evening was finally within reach.

The Airbnb Paula had booked for that evening was a small chalet located on a small private lake just off the Rue de Pailleuse, close to the town center of Castets. The location was extremely serene and pretty, and the chalet was modern and clean inside with large sliding French doors that opened onto a glorious deck that overlooked the water. We walked the dogs around the lake in the late afternoon sunshine. It was pretty and cool by the water, lined by bullrushes, bright green stalks, and cottonwool-colored seed heads, all framed by tall poplars that threw refreshing shade over the scene. The water itself though was murky, not clean enough to let Archie and Pi have a swim and there were dense dark clouds of midges that hovered over the middle of the lake.

The three of us walked back into town across an ancient bridge that spanned a sparkling river full of water lilies. It could have been the spot that inspired Monet, so pretty and quintessentially French. We picked up the evening's dinner and supplies for the next few days from a supermarket we had passed on the way in. Back at the chalet we drank cold beers and ate fat juicy pink shrimp on the deck and joked and laughed and enjoyed the last of the sunshine together.

Adam went to his room early. Paula and I had a last drink and then, weary from another long day on the road Paula also headed to bed. A shriek from the bedroom had me running to see what the problem was. The bedroom was full of black, biting midges. Every surface, floor, walls, and ceiling painted black by their teeming, writhing forms. Paula loathes insects and here they numbered in the tens, perhaps hundreds of thousands. As evening fell, the lights from the chalet must have drawn them from the lake, through the French doors of the bedroom which we had earlier mistakenly opened to air the room.

I searched for the vacuum cleaner, it was located in the wardrobe, an ancient red Henry with a hose for a nose and a painted and ironically cheery grinning expression. I dragged a chair into the room and started to vacuum the bugs. It took over an hour to completely remove all the midges. The walls and ceiling needed to be repeatedly vacuumed as they re-formed constantly behind our cleaning efforts. At one point it appeared they were still finding entry to the bedroom and we were losing the battle, but we finally broke their hold over the room, and with one last run around with my new pal Henry, the job was done. Our sleep that night was troubled, tiny insectoid bodies crawling and creeping through our dreams.

Viva Espana

July 4th, 2020

Adam was taking a shower when we woke up the next morning. He was confused by sleep, wondering why the bathroom was full of dead bugs. His room had escaped the invasion of the midges and he was blissfully unaware of the excitement in the bedroom next door. Adam walked Archie and Pi around the lake while we packed the car. The dogs were reluctant to jump back into the car, but I was pretty excited to get going. By the end of today's drive, we should be in Northern Spain and only one more day's drive from the villa. It would also be my first time crossing the Pyrenees. On the European motorcycle trips of my youth, I had never visited Spain, preferring the Alps of France, Austria, and Northern Italy.

Our destination today was the small village of Bellmunt D'Urgell situated in Northern Catalonia. The morning's drive would take us first eastward and parallel to the Spanish border before we passed the town of Lourdes, famed for its healing waters, and headed south for the ascent into the mountains. The morning was overcast with sporadic drops of rain which kept the temperature in the car to reasonable levels. As we skirted the eleventh-century town of Pau, the dark and jagged skyline of the French Pyrenees hove into sight for the first time. Soon it filled the entire panorama, the ten-thousand-foot peaks of Pic du Midi d'Ossau and Vignemale soared ominously above the horizon.

The Pyrenees themselves unfold for over three hundred miles, from the Cantabrian Mountains close to the Atlantic coast all the way across to the Mediterranean Sea. Separating Spain from France, the area is truly vast, encompassing multiple mountain peaks, with over a hundred being in excess of ten thousand feet. There are very few passes across the mountain range and those that do exist are at unusually high elevations. The crossing presented a challenge, but it was summer, the weather was benevolent, and snow-free, and so far, we had made good progress in the old Mondeo.

We chose the route along the Garonne River, coincidentally the same river we had crossed in Bordeaux the previous day. Rather than wide and slow as it is toward the coastal estuary, closer to its source it is fast-flowing, white-flecked, twisting and babbling over the granite rocks and pebbles. The first part of the journey was a pleasant meander through the valley, verdant meadows filled with summer flowers, purple orchids, and alpine white saxifrages. The initial ascent was a gentle and easy drive.

We stopped to stretch our legs and share a measly lunch at a layby just north of the tiny town of Arlos, just a few miles short of the French border with Spain. A French couple, well dressed, but elderly, were already seated at the only picnic table. A veritable stereotype, they were both drinking red wine and eating bread and cheese. We had a warm coke and a couple of cold meat pies stood around the car, nobody wanting to sit for a while. We watered the dogs and took a comfort break in the trees by the side of the road. The day was beautiful and below us, through the canopy, we could hear the noisy Garonne River as it churned its way down the mountainside.

At the Pont de Rei, the bridge across the Garonne that marks the open border between France and Spain, we had only climbed twenty-five hundred feet. But the snow-blanketed peak of Pico Aneto, the highest mountain in the Pyrenees could be occasionally glimpsed between the conifer-blanketed hills that flanked the valley. A stern and ominous reminder of the steep and long climb ahead. We crossed the Garonne once more and, at last, we were in Spain. We all gave a small half-hearted cheer as we passed the border marker and the road signs shifted into Spanish.

We were now in the Val d'Aran, a valley once closed off to the rest of Spain during the harsh winter months prior to the opening of the Vielha tunnel in 1948. Displaying once more our uncanny ability to pick the worst of any given option, it was toward the tunnel we were heading. It was once the longest tunnel in the world, three and a half miles long at an elevation of over five thousand feet. Unknown to us at the time, we discovered later that due to its appalling lack of emergency facilities, it was also known as the most dangerous tunnel in Europe.

Into the mouth of the tunnel

Crags and peaks surrounded us on both sides as we continued to climb through turns and switchbacks. The town of Vielha itself was on our left in a deep cut of a valley below us. A steep left curve swept us over the river Nere and then we passed the exit bore of the old tunnel, still used to transport dangerous or flammable goods. Then the black mouth of the tunnel entrance, framed by the towering snowy peaks of Pico Aneto on the left and Pico Mulleres on the right, swallowed us. Despite its three lanes, it felt narrow, dimly lit, and oppressive. The tunnel is driven through the mountainside, five thousand feet of rock above us. The weight of the mountain above was manifest and the road climbed endlessly, not insanely steep, but mile after grueling, grinding mile, a steady gradient, always upwards.

Suddenly we were concerned. The temperature gauge on the old Mondeo was starting to inch toward the red zone. The length of the tunnel meant there was little fresh air circulating, overwhelming the aging engine's ability to cool effectively and there was nowhere I could see to pull over to allow the engine to cool. The gauge was now hard into the red zone and we were still climbing. With tendrils of steam starting to rise from the bonnet in front of us, the only option appeared to be to pull over by the side of the road, into the darkness and hope for rescue before we caused a collision. Just as we indicated our intention, ahead in the far distance, around a bend to the left there was the proverbial gleam of sunlight. We were through.

The shadow of Pico Aneto was thankfully behind us, and on the other side of the tunnel, the landscape had changed immensely. While on the French side, the geography and flora were almost alpine, lush, and fertile, here on the Spanish side the climate was Mediterranean, rocky with shades of grey and umber, where avalanches and tree falls had created scree fields replacing previous expanses of forestation.

We were also immediately descending, down from the highest point of the pass, the Mondeo engine was quickly cooling in the mountain air, the needle dropping once more back into its normal range. The foothills of the Pyrenees are almost entirely located on the Spanish side, created eighty million years ago by the slow, deliberate tectonic collision of the Iberian peninsula into the solid landmass of what is now Southern France. Crumpling the landscape before it into the increasingly lofty heights that formed around the modern border. The mountains are still steep and lofty and stretch far into the distance, but the road cuts through them in a natural valley, carved by the Noguera Ribagorcana River as it snakes parallel to the road, emptying noisily into the Canelles reservoir ahead of us, a vast cold splash of milky azure within the arid landscape. The road ahead was a series of fast-sweeping bends flanked by lofty Pinsapo Pines, and we made fast, fun progress as we headed for the valley floor and the province of Lleida.

The heat of the Spanish summer was already making itself evident as we lost elevation and descended toward the plain, and the interior of the car was again uncomfortably hot, but we had avoided the highways and we lowered the car windows to create a more comfortable cross breeze. It felt incredible to finally be in Spain and through the Pyrenees. Every mile we completed brought us closer to not only tonight's respite but tomorrow's goal of Altea.

We stopped for gas on the outskirts of Alfarras, a small market town located on the banks of the Noguera Ribagorcana. The garage owner was a friendly sun-darkened Catalan who spoke wonderful English, having worked and studied in Portsmouth of all places, in his youth. Pumping gas with a cigarette in his hand he warned us that Lleida, the town only twenty miles ahead had been put into a complete lockdown that morning, due to a renewed outbreak of COVID-19. The Guardia Civil was restricting movement and not allowing anybody to enter or leave. He counseled us that we should avoid the area if we could.

On the road for three days, we had been insulated by travel from both news and most human contact. Pick up a key for an Airbnb, a quick stop for groceries or gas. These had been our only interactions. It was a hard reminder that in the towns we were passing through, and those we were still to reach, Governments and communities were still fighting the spread and effects of the disease.

The drive was flat and easy, for the most part, the road was ours alone, perhaps influenced by the limits on free movement. We had entered the Catalan Central Depression, a series of ancient, eroded river basins. The landscape was almost Martian in appearance, flat for as far as the eye could see, edged by scrub and rendered red ochre and mustard brown by the clay sediments deposited here ten thousand millennia ago. We prudently and carefully picked our way around the quarantined town of Lleida and finally approached Bellmunt d'Urgell, our destination for the night. The first sight was the small bell tower of the church of St. Josep which rises from the flat dusty ochre of the shimmering Spanish plain proclaiming the presence of the town, home to less than two hundred inhabitants. The village is tiny, a hamlet really, comprised of a few dozen homes huddled together on a rocky peninsula. The ascent was steep with crazy tight turns leading to our home for the night.

We were early and had to wait for the young property owner to arrive with the key. The house had a garage, an ancient cellar, dark, wet, and cold, carved into the hillside upon which sat the home. Inside it was cool and clean; we had been fortunate with the properties we had rented so far. There was no local store or restaurant, and with the nearby towns in quarantine, we were loath to venture back out, so we cooled beers and shared what food we had remaining.

Our Spanish Villa and the start of our new life lay three hundred miles south of us, five hours drive away. Paula texted Jim and Maria to let them know when we would be arriving so they could meet us there. After all of our planning and re-planning, the last-minute flights, the long quarantine, and the journey across Europe it was finally within reach. Paula and I slept well that night, happy that our move to Spain was soon to be accomplished, arriving at our haven where we could rest and take stock, time on our hands to figure out the next stage of our lives together.

Arrival

July 5th, 2020

    An amber dawn streamed through the meager curtains of the bedroom that Sunday morning and the bells from the church behind us pealed, strangely muted, and hushed across the rooftops. It was already warm, but we took the time to walk the pups around the village. We wondered, not for the first time that week, what the locals of a place like this did for fun and employment. Our elevation from the top of the village extended us views for miles across the heat-shimmering plain below. The only obvious place of work was at the base of the hill, the rising squeals, and aromas indicating a pig farm or possible abattoir.

    The car loaded, we set off back down the hill and southeast toward Tarragona. It was late morning by the time we got to the coast and saw for the first time the Mediterranean dazzling under the glare of the sun. It was already sweltering in the car. We were driving directly into the sun and it just couldn't be escaped. Adam jammed pillows and clothes against the rear windows in an attempt to keep the sun off the dogs, but the temperature inside continued to rise. North of Valencia we were forced to stop at a service station and put the dogs in the shade. We got cold water and poured it over them to relieve their stress.

    We were only two hours from Altea, but the sun was still relentlessly rising. It wasn't only the dogs who were suffering. We had lived in Atlanta, in the deep south of the USA for fourteen years, but the heat of that Spanish summer literally took our breath away. We really had no option but to press on and keep splashing the dogs with the increasingly warm water from the bottles we had filled.

    We passed the towns of Castellon de la Plana and Port de Sagunt, and then the port city of Valencia, a glint of church towers set amid the heavy industrial heart of the city, dark ocean freighters moored, queueing patiently out at sea. Slowly the miles slipped by and finally more familiar towns started to appear on the exit signs. First Denia, then Xabia, and at last Calpe the last town north of Altea. Our excitement at arriving was somewhat tempered by the suffocation of the car, but from the highway, we could occasionally steal a glimpse of the familiar blue-domed church that stands high above the town of Altea. Finally, the last sign for our exit, and then we were heading toward the villa.

Turning off the highway was a huge relief, we immediately wound all the windows down. There was a modicum of relief but even the breeze from the Sea to our left was scorching. We skirted the town center, busy with families heading to the beaches, and then upwards into the hills behind. The roads narrowed to little more than dusty dirt tracks and we were often forced to pull over, skirting stone white-washed walls to let trucks and other cars past. Never having visited the Villa, we were following the navigation blindly and the road seemed to go on interminably, turn after turn.

At last, we passed a decrepit church, over the crest of a hill, past an empty dilapidated home with white paint peeling, one more hairpin, and the villa lay before us at the end of a long stretch of dusty crumbling asphalt. Thick adobe walls the color of champagne topped by blue mosaic tile, framed by purple and white bougainvillea, all under the reach of a towering palm. The electric sliding gate was standing open and the owners of the villa were inside waiting for us. I parked the Mondeo, engine cooling, ticking, and popping, under the palm tree by the swimming pool, and we all slowly uncoiled from our seats, clothing soaked and muscles cramping.

The owners of the Villa, Jim and his Spanish wife Maria were dashing around the house, simultaneously packing, fussing, and cleaning. Jim had been stranded in the villa since March by the state of alarm imposed by the Spanish government, and Maria had joined him only the week prior to our arrival. Despite three months-notice and calls and texts to update them of progress on our trip across Europe, it was as if we had turned up on their doorstep unannounced. However, we knew that they were newly reunited and themselves preparing for a drive back to their home in Belgium. All we really wanted was some solitude to recover from the heat of the drive and to discover our new surroundings ourselves, but with the dogs watered and cooling down in the air conditioning, we were prepared to be polite and patient.

I listened to Jim's garbled and confusing explanations of how the pool, garden irrigation, TV, AC, and water heating systems worked. I could see Adam smirking at me behind his back, sensing my frustration. This was partly because Jim had promised to write all the instructions down prior to our arrival, which he had not, and also because he was scatterbrained, jumping from system to system, one to the other. I had stopped listening to his endless nonsensical diatribe and decided I would figure it out for myself through trial and error over the next few days.

Eventually, with final farewells, last shouted instructions, and slamming of car doors, they were gone. We let out a collective sigh of relief, grabbed a cold Heineken, and prepared for a dip in the pool. First, we quickly explored the house. The older part of the original house was roomy and dark, Spanish designed and built, with thick walls to retain the natural cool of the stone. It had a large open entry vestibule with entry to the front of the property, a staircase to the left, and one ground floor En-suite bedroom accessed by a door below the stairs. This would be Adam's room. The main living room was to the right of this staircase, and through the living room was what had been used as a dining room, then another room which seemed to be used as storage, and then onto the open modern kitchen. Beyond the kitchen was a more modern and light extension which was used as a gymnasium and office, as well as a laundry room at the far end. Upstairs there were another three bedrooms, the master being En-suite, which would be ours, and one family bathroom that overlooked the olive fields at the back.

Back at the pool, we drank a cold beer and started to relax. We don't remember much of the remainder of that first day. Ecstatic, relieved to have finally, safely arrived. It seemed an eternity in the planning and a similar timeframe in the execution, but here we were. I took some photos to send to family and close friends to let them know we had safely arrived, and a few more to post to Facebook, to show people our life was better than theirs. My favorite is of Adam holding one of those small calendars you can use to manually flip the numbers to count down the days to a special event, the birth of a baby, wedding, anniversary, arrival in a foreign country after a desperate journey across a virally infected continent, that sort of thing.

We had set it back at the beginning of the year to countdown the days until we would arrive at the Villa. I am looking at the photo now. Adam looks hot and weary, a Florida gator's cap on backward, his beard straggled and overgrown, blue eyes crossed, staring into the middle distance, his T-shirt is stained, disheveled, and damp with sweat. He is standing outside by the pool, half illuminated by late afternoon sunshine, his right hand is holding a Heineken, and the figures on the countdown calendar held in his left are "Day – 0000."

We had made it...

Arrived

First Day

July 6th, 2020

In the morning, I awoke, unable to sleep. The room was still dark, but above the window shutter by our bed, a faint light was painting a slow arc across the ceiling. I got up quietly and went down, alone, outside to the pool. The pre-dawn of that first Spanish morning was chilly, the garden silent, flora and fauna together lamenting the soon-to-be-lost cool of the night and readying themselves in anticipation of the coming brutal heat of the day.

Looking out across the pool and over the lemon trees I could just make out the silhouette of the huge limestone outcrop of Peñón de Ifach, jutting out into the Sea, dominating the coastal town of Calpe, black against the dark purple of the Mediterranean.

The sun first threw light on the water as it rose, still hidden to sight behind the limestone, purples faded to navy, cobalts to sapphire. The sky brightened in a dawn half-light and then the sun broke cover from behind the limestone peaks. The landscape was immediately illuminated and the cool and silence of the night was tempered by the warmth of the sun and the sound of insects. Another sultry day was on its way.

Later, we ate breakfast together by the pool, orange juice, and pate on crusty bread under the cover of a Moorish veranda. There was welcome shade and a large dining table, cast iron with a warped and hand-hewn oak tabletop. Bougainvillea grew rampant against the villa walls. Hibiscus, Hypericum, and Oleander surrounded the lemon trees behind the pool. Pomegranates and Kumquats were girdled by succulents and cacti against the garden walls. The views everywhere were truly breathtaking. The azure Mediterranean sparkled and twinkled in the distance, framed by the colossal rock of Calpe to our left and the crystal blue dome of the church that soared above the whitewashed jumble of houses of the old town to our right. A natural buttress four thousand feet high, the Sierra de Bernia mountain range wrapped the rear of this panorama coast to coast, encircled us and the town of Altea, constantly changing in shadow and hue as the earth rotated, cycled the sun across the cloudless sky.

The sea in the distance, beyond the town below us, was spectacular, but it was the mountains that drew the eye throughout each hour of every day. The view changed minute by minute as clouds slipped by and the height of the sun threw different shadows across the rocks, exposed bluffs, crevices, and caves. The distance faded the dark brown and black crags to a misty gray and the heat haze shimmered the light across every tor and pinnacle. They were constantly, outstandingly beautiful.

The rest of the day we pottered and explored, unpacked our few things and took our first real look at the Villa, the place we would count as home for at least the next three to six months.

The first thing we noticed was the spiders, Spanish Salticidae, or jumping spiders. Small but swift and impossible to catch, they would leap in your direction when you tried to swat them away, making us jump in return. They were all over both the interior and exterior of the villa, on stairs, in cupboards, drawers, and tabletops. Then the cobwebs, once the eye caught sight of one, the rest were brought into sharp focus. Draping dust covered the gossamer threads above us, slung from lights and across windows. Despite Jim having been trapped in the villa for months, and the apparent frenzied cleaning efforts by Maria when we arrived, everything was filthy. We definitely brought some American sensibilities and expectations with us, but the villa was not cheap to rent and even the Airbnb's on route had been more sanitary.

The other thing that became apparent throughout the day was that we were now living in a house owned by folks with a borderline hoarding disorder. Personal pictures and photographs coated every inch of every wall, every draw in every room was filled with random, often useless broken items, old board games, and jigsaws, all with pieces missing were crammed onto shelves. Games consoles, but no games, box after box of tangled cables and incompatible adapters. Every space on the many bookcases was packed, stocked high with books and magazines. The kitchen was the same. A hundred mugs and glasses were stored in the racks above the worktops, each one grimy and stained, not a single one matching another but some with the occasional bonus of a tiny, desiccated spider corpse. Every shelf in every cupboard in the kitchen cabinets was filled with kitchen tools and utensils, mismatched cutlery, blunt carving knives, blenders and graters, slicers, and dicers. The freezer was full of unwrapped and freezer-burnt bread, probably panic-bought by Jim when he initially got locked down but crumbling and useless now. The shelves of the pantry were stocked with jars of jams, pickles, and sauces, every single one opened, partly used, and far beyond their expiry date. The fridge was half stocked with cheese and butter, milk, and juice. Nothing was new or sealed.

Then the furniture. Couches and chairs, ottomans and beanbags, chaises and recliners, coffee tables, side tables, and nesting tables. Furniture everywhere. Personal clothing items too, all left behind and discarded, randomly stored in wardrobes, cupboards, and on coat racks for us to find. Perhaps they thought we might be in need of a spare pair of dirty flip-flops, a hat with a broad but broken brim, or should there be a cold snap, a disheveled, floor-length ladies' dressing gown.

We hadn't brought many possessions with us on the journey, but we still couldn't find a place to store them. It was all a little bizarre.

Life in Spain

July 2020

 We spent the next few days re-arranging and moving furniture and bits and pieces to get the villa into a more livable space; we stored excess furniture and vase after vase of hideous, fake, and dusty flowers in a ramshackle, ant-infested outbuilding adjacent to the house. We emptied the contents of the pantry, freezers, and refrigerators into some black kitchen sacks we found under the sink and had Adam walk them down to the communal trash collection area by the decrepit church.

 I spent days trying to figure out the garden irrigation system and the timing of the pool pumps. I slowly figured out that turning something simple into something with unnecessary complexity was Jim's adopted vocation. Everything that required a wire or a connection to another thing was ineptly over-engineered. Every other day I was on hands and knees in the dark and creature-infested ramshackle lean-to behind the outbuilding, with a torch between my teeth tweaking the idiosyncratic, cross-connected, and complex timing mechanisms. The pool pumps continued to turn on at a different time each day, sometimes with a ferocious flow that made the water churn and heave, and on other days with such a puny flow it was hard to tell they were running at all. At least I got the pool pumps to run. As far as I could tell the irrigation system never once worked and I ended up watering the gorgeous garden with the hosepipe, determined not to let its beauty wither in the heat.

 After finally getting the pumps to somewhat circulate, I noticed that the pool was fitted with an auto-filling valve. Like a toilet cistern, a float inside holds the incoming water off when the pool is full. As the water level drops the float opens the valve and tops off the pool. It never worked. The tremendous heat of the day and the burning sun evaporated a huge amount of water every day, you could almost see the pool level drop. It would have been great if the auto filler had worked but it was no big deal, I just manually topped the pool level off each day with the hose pipe after the plants had been watered. Until the night the auto-filler decided to burst surprisingly into life, while we were all asleep, and failed to turn off when the pool was filled. I woke to find the yard flooded and water still gushing in through the inlet. I called Jim and he said not to worry, he would contact his pool guy, Jose, who would be around immediately. Jose never did turn up, so I ended up simply jamming a pebble under the float mechanism. It's probably still like that now.

Every TV needed four remotes to work, amplifiers, satellite boxes, and smart TVs all connected with a tangle of cables and all co-dependent on each other to operate. Despite Jim's claim of satellite, and the physical evidence of the boxes, we could never find anything other than three Spanish news channels, so we unplugged everything that wasn't needed, bought a Firestick, and subscribed to a UK TV service.

Two of the air conditioning units in the house didn't work. The one in the gym, really just a sunny room with an exercise bike in it, looked beyond repair but the one in the main part of the house rattled loudly, didn't cool effectively, and constantly dripped condensation onto the floor of the living room. The rattle sounded terminal, a failing bearing, or something similar. I called the maintenance company Jim had recommended we use for general problems, and in my best Spanish described the problem.

"It is too noisy much, too many waters, no is cold."

The guy came round the next day and after parking his van and diligently unloading small tools, dragged a step ladder under the unit and hit it really hard with the side of a yard brush that had been leaned up by the door under the unit. The rattling and the dripping water stopped immediately. Now we knew what the brush was there for we kept it handy.

There were three toilets in the house and not a single one functioned correctly. A knob on the top of the cistern was pulled to flush and on most occasions, even with the gentlest of pulls, the user would be left both surprised and disappointed, with an unemptied toilet and a knob in their hand. I spent an inefficient, if finally productive day, rifling through the drawers of the villa to find suitable wires and pliers, and with some experimentation managed to jury rig each one to function correctly.

While searching for toilet repairing provisions, we found a drinks cabinet in the dark and gloomy room behind the kitchen. Bottles of ancient Cinzano, Disaronno, Bacardi, Campari, Grand Marnier, and Harvey's Bristol Cream sherry. A veritable clinking and dusty hostelry, a throwback from the 1970s, each bottle had been opened, and somewhat consumed. It was all stored in the outbuilding with the rest of the crap and locked away. We wouldn't be tempted to drink it, but Adam wasn't famous at that time for demonstrating consistently good judgment, and that amount of bygone booze would turn him blind if it didn't kill him.

We were slowly figuring the villa and its puzzling array of contents out and making it work for us.

Running low on provisions, we drove into town and stocked up on groceries. It was really fun shopping in the Spanish supermarket, aptly named Mas y Mas (More and More). Masks and hand sanitizer were required, and plastic gloves had to be worn to handle produce. The gloves were so thin and cheap that fingers went straight through, but the sentiment was valid, and we appreciated the precautions. There was the mix of familiar and foreign, the feeling you get when you are on vacation in Europe, except now we were actually living here.

British Pot Noodles and Hob Nob biscuits lay cheek by jowl alongside, well, cheeks and jowls. Packaging with Spanish words we didn't understand yet, not aided by the bizarre cartoon-like pictures presumably describing the contents. The Spanish beer was as cheap as the bottled water. I found a bottle of red wine for sixty cents and was deliriously happy.

The fruit and vegetables were wonderfully natural and fresh, odd-shaped, and miscolored the way they are found in nature. The oranges were delicious, as were the ripe pomegranates, figs, and quince. The incredible climate created a wealth of freshness and availability.

Then the hams. We gorged for weeks on the Spanish hams. Catholicism may be dominant in Spain, but the worship of the noble Cerdo comes close. In the supermarkets, whole legs of serrano are hung from stands ready to purchase. There are Secreto Iberico, Presa Iberica, Arbizu Chistorra, Casa Noguera Botifarra Negra, Morcilla, Lomo Embuchado, and a hundred varieties of Chorizo. Just from the Iberian region, there is Jamon Iberico Cebo de Campo and Jamon Iberico de Recebo. The champagne of hams, so to speak is Jamon Iberico de Bellota, the meat for this rich and delicious cut is derived from pigs that live free range in the woods, feeding only on wild acorns. The selection was enormous, and over the next few weeks, we would eat our way through many of them. Pound upon pound of salty ham was surely beneficial for high blood pressure, right?

The next stop was at the local linen store on the Partida Cap-Blanch. Given the general cleanliness of the villa, Paula thought new clean bedspreads and sheets might be prudent. The store owners were English and helped us convert the sizes to fit Spanish bed measurements. We bought some new towels, bright blue, soft and fleecy, from the same place. It's often the smallest of things, the nods towards normality, that make somewhere feel homely.

We drove back through town and headed back into the hills. Starting to get a sense of direction and layout of the town, we didn't need navigation all the time which made us both feel more settled. Back at the villa we unpacked our groceries and took the new fluffy towels and bedding upstairs. Stripping the bed of its existing sheets revealed the mattress, a giant Jim-shaped stain, crime scene brown was spread across the side of the bed I had been sleeping on.

One of the things we remembered fondly from our first trip in November was the food, and since we arrived in Altea we had been excited to return to Quarara, our favorite restaurant where we previously ate amazing steaks.

We walked along the hot dusty road from the villa toward the old town. The villa was isolated with only a handful of neighbors. Secured from the street by a tall steel gate that was electrically operated from inside, the track outside the gates was narrow with a steep drop off into the lemon grove below us. Twisting its way between fan palms, citrus groves, and large flowering hibiscus, reds, and blues lined our path. We set off in high spirits, telling Adam he was in for a culinary treat of epic proportions; excited to re-visit both the old town and to re-live the experience of the wonderful hospitality and fresh ingredients cooked by Marco and his team.

The walk took us past the decrepit church we had passed on the way into the villa. It is the venue of an annual festival in late August in celebration of Saint Lluis, but when we explored, it was desolate and in ruins, with no sign of life left to be seen. Early evening hadn't brought a respite from the torrid heat of the day, the roads reflected the captured warmth back up toward us, even as the sun began to set behind the mountains.

Our map showed us a shortcut, which took us down a rapidly narrowing avenue between decrepit-looking houses, over a small bridge that spanned a dry riverbed and down a steep bank toward a drainage channel which we crossed on slippery stepping-stones. The track is overgrown with scrubby weeds and zigzags between ramshackle houses. As we passed the first house our surprise appearance startled the obligatory guard dog. It charged the fence, barking and snarling ferociously, yellow teeth bared and slaver flying in our direction.

Now alarmed and on alert, our arrival at each property was met with already barking dogs, some chained but most threw themselves hard against the rattling chain-linked fences, snarling menacingly and running the property line snapping at our passing. We sure hoped the owners were keeping these fences in good repair.

The walk up through the old town was steep, the narrow, cobbled streets turned left and right as they led us in a twisted, upwards toward the church, the Parroquia Nuestra Senora del Consuelo at the very top. The restaurant was still there, tucked away in the square behind the church, just as we remembered.

Arriving breathless, parched, and sweaty, but hungry, we asked for Marco, but he was no longer there. Having fled the virus, he had returned home to be with his family in Italy. Apparently, he had taken the good food and service with him.

We ordered a starter to share and were scolded that this wasn't possible. The waiters were churlish, and so were the steaks. Tough and overcooked, the meat was awful, and the sauces we had savored from our previous visits, were thin, insipid, and lacking in flavor. We walked home a little saddened, the sun had set, and the darkness was falling across the plain before us. We tiptoed in silence, back along the track, careful not to disturb the slumbering guard dogs.

We had lunches under shady yellow parasols by the rocky beach in the town of Altea. The Mediterranean Sea close to shore was an unrealistic blue, a shade of turquoise so vivid that if painted it would appear ridiculous, a clumsy error by the artist. Further out, the sea darkened but remained a startlingly bright aqua-marine, dotted with the pretty white sails of fishing boats from the harbor to our south, and reflecting the clear cerulean sky above. The food in town was more varied, we tried sushi and Thai as well as the good and varied choice of traditional Spanish cuisine. The Tapas and sandwiches were good but not what we remembered from our first visit. Adam was shocked when he ordered a five-euro Coke and received a tiny, infant-sized bottle and no free refill.

This was to become an unfortunate theme. The virus had subtly changed the town, every bar and restaurant a little less accommodating, every interaction a little less pleasant. The food we remembered as being fresh and delicious was mostly mediocre and disappointing.

The one remarkable meal we had was at the local Indian restaurant. We love Indian food, but across the world, the restaurants somehow manage to seamlessly and consistently evoke flock wallpaper and twangy sitar music, Bollywood movies playing on ancient TVs in the background. This place was not so different, apart from the views.

We followed our somewhat surly waiter, up four twisting flights of steep stone steps and walked out onto the top of the world, or at least as high in

Altea as it is possible to be. The blue ceramic dome of the church in the Casco Antiguo felt within touching distance and the Mediterranean was spread out like an azure carpet far below us. The meal itself was full of spice and flavor and the lamb was delicious, and obviously derived from a sheep, which isn't always the case.

The Spanish attitude to the virus was impressive, and the wearing of masks specifically. On our trip from the US to the UK and then across France, nobody was as diligent as the Spanish. In town, everybody wore a mask, everywhere, both inside the stores and outside walking on the narrow streets and broad squares. There was mutual respect and a sense that the civil obedience of the recent months had collectively saved the lives of many. The Spanish death rate had been the highest in the world, not necessarily here in sleepy Altea, the epicenter of fatalities had occurred in the large, populous, and crowded urban centers of Madrid and Barcelona. Regardless, the Spanish had taken note and to the largest extent silently but mutually agreed to fight the spread of infection together. There was no doubt that this was aided by the Guardia Civil who enforced the rules quickly, politely but strictly. Smiling couples taking selfies, faces uncovered just for a moment, high above the Mediterranean in the Plaza de Iglesia, were dealt with by the Guardia. We felt safer in Spain than anywhere else on our trip.

More Life in Spain

July 2020

During those first weeks, we met Sophie in the coffee bar of the Hotel Villa Dagea, tall, pretty, and immaculately dressed, Sophie was a local Spanish lawyer who would be helping us with our residency certification. With Brexit on the horizon and the separation of the UK from the European Union, we needed to get all the paperwork completed quickly in order to be able to stay in the country. We hired a lawyer because Spanish Bureaucracy is, frankly, the worst in the world, and while we had basic conversational Spanish at this point (thanks Duo), our ability to communicate complex matters with government agencies was zero. We had tried ourselves to get even simple forms completed at the local banks, but every submission came with a frown and a shrug and the response "no es correcto" or "no es possible," and of course we lacked the Spanish to question why.

The worst part of Spain is that the rules and procedures are intentionally complex and obfuscated but are also openly interpreted in different ways by every agency in every region. Each government official, once appointed to office and suitably indentured receives a pen protector, a scowl, and the gift of turning a government mandate into a personal opinion.

On a visit to the police station in Benidorm, to file paperwork for the Padron, or Empadronamiento as it is properly known, the paperwork required to remain permanently in the country, even our lawyer fell victim to the whims of the presiding official. Part of the application required that we prove means, that we had sufficient money to be able to live without incurring government financial assistance while we resided in Spain. The law clearly states that the money can be in any bank account anywhere in the world. Ours was clearly still in the United States, as we couldn't open a Spanish bank account without the bloody paperwork we had visited the police station in Benidorm that morning to receive.

It didn't matter that we were represented by Sophie with her grandiose law degree and her native Spanish language skills, the junior clerk on duty that day demanded that we show proof of funds in a Spanish bank and was not to be persuaded otherwise. Frustrated, we left. Sophie's advice was that we be patient and try a different police station, this time in Alicante, where she was sure we would get an opinion more aligned with the actual law.

At the same time, we were still using the costly cell phones we had brought from the US and needed to get them swapped out for Spanish phones and contracts. It proved to be impossible. To take out a Spanish cell phone contract a Spanish bank account is needed. We couldn't get the bank account without the Padron, and the Padron required the bank account.

The same with the car, the Mondeo was a liability in Spain. The air conditioning was still broken, and the roads were too tight and twisting to navigate easily or safely. Even when we arrived at any destination there was seldom a space big enough for the big estate car. We wanted to swap the Mondeo for a tiny Fiat. Cash is king in the United States, but not in Spain. Car dealers in Spain can't sell a car to anybody without a Padron and...yeah you guessed it.

I am sure Sophie would have eventually prevailed, but endless circulatory and conflicting reasoning plague the mañana driven system, it was tiresome and frustrating.

On the subject of tiresome and frustrating, what is wrong with Spanish air conditioning? Enter a bank, business, or store in the United States in the summer months and you better hope you have brought a sweater, scarf, and perhaps some mittens. The air conditioning there evokes conditions similar to the Arctic. All buildings in Spain have air conditioning and it's every bit as hot as the United States outside, if not more so. Air conditioning in Spain just doesn't work. We waited for hours in government buildings and offices, waiting on officials to complete paperwork, listening to the background hum of air conditioning units but not benefiting from a single cool waft, while sitting in steadily spreading pools of perspiration.

Amazon deliveries were also tiresome and frustrating. Not the ordering on the website, that's refreshingly similar, better actually, as picking the items you want in Spanish adds a frisson of excitement and uncertainty to every selection. It's the delivery we never figured out. Sure, the villa was remote, but it had an actual address and could be easily found on Google Maps. Hell, even we found it! The delivery drivers however could not.

It always started the same, one of our phones would ring with a Madrid area code on the display. Our hearts would sink, and the caller would speak rapidly in Spanish, mostly unintelligible to us until we picked out a couple of familiar key words and realized they were asking where we were.

Given the driver had a parcel, with the actual address written on the front, and presumably a phone or other navigational aid, why couldn't the two be put together in some productive way? We never figured out why it was so challenging for them and ended up storing a URL to the villa's location, taken from Google Maps and stored on our phones, which we could quickly text or WhatsApp to the driver.

Our Spanish language skills were slowly improving though. I supplemented Duolingo with textbooks and YouTube clips. The audio clips were the most useful to me at that juncture. I could read in Spanish surprisingly well and could ask for most things that I wanted, albeit speaking like a toddler held back from progression to first grade by a combination of learning difficulties and a speech impediment. It was the responses I couldn't understand.

The problem lay not in the vocabulary, but much more in the insisted celerity of the speaker. Every Spanish native spoke with Gatling gun velocity. It's like the Spanish populace has all entered into some twisted competition, where prizes are awarded to the player who utters the most words per minute, with bonuses given for the ability to run the words and syllables together into one extended but admittedly beautiful-sounding sentence. We simply couldn't translate at that pace and "hable más despacio por favor" had little effect.

Paula and I always traveled together, pack-like, when we needed to be understood. We figured out that speaking and listening required two different parts of the brain. At least when first learning a foreign language was concerned, when one was engaged in speaking, the listening half was rendered both deaf and altogether dumb. Together though we were a gifted double act, the oratory and auditory equivalent of a veritable Fred Astaire and Ginger Rogers, or at least the Krankies. Paula would speak and I would translate the response, or vice versa. We would look at each other for a moment and consolidate our results, and if successful we would move on to the next part of the conversation.

By the way, don't let anybody tell you that if you speak English, you will be just fine in Spain. Perhaps that works in the tourist towns of Benidorm or the large English communities around Los Alcazares, but in most of Spain, the Spanish speak precisely one language. They speak it incredibly well, and they are justified and correct in not needing to know yours but don't expect much help when you show up without practice or a phrase book.

Even More Life in Spain

July 2020

As the days slipped by, getting around was becoming a challenge. The heat was fiercely unrelenting, and the villa was just far enough into the hills that every walk to the town or to the beach was turned into a trial of dusty de-hydration. The big Mondeo had been a boon on the long overland journey across Europe, but in the backwaters of Spain, it was a devil to drive around the country roads, so tight and twisty, every turn a heart-jumping surprise. On one hot trip to the supermarket, we stopped by the church to dispose of some garbage bags in the communal waste area and when we started the car again, for no apparent reason, all of the parking sensor alarms came on at full, high-pitched blaring volume.

Nothing I did could turn them off, and we were forced to drive to the supermarket with the windows down, stressed and deafened by the incessant screaming blare, NEEP, NEEP, NEEP, of the warning signal. Startled locals we passed stared as the three red-faced English strangers drove by in their rusty blue Spanish car, going, NEEP, NEEP, NEEP, as it went. When I got the car back to the villa, I found the fuse that powered the sensors, extracted it, and hurled it with a ferocity that surprised even me, over the garden wall.

The wall of bureaucracy meant we still couldn't sell it to buy a tiny Fiat so we hired a little scooter which was way more practical and fun. It made trips into town for shopping, or to the seaside for lunch or dinner so much easier. Paula and Adam both had wobbly scooter practice on the dusty roads outside the villa, making me anxious every time they went out of sight and remained so for more than a minute or so. The hot air of the day was even cooled a little by the speed of the little bike.

We drove the scooter down to the market that took place on a Tuesday morning. I had a favorite parking spot, a little cluster of parking spaces reserved for bikes outside the Il Timone pizza takeaway. The market square was opposite and on most days was Altea's largest car park, just off the Partida Basseta. On market day, with all normal parking spaces consumed by the market itself, the town was madly congested. With the scooter parked and helmets locked under the seat, we strolled across to check out the famous market, the largest on the Costa Blanca for ourselves. I wouldn't say it was awful, there was just not much there. Leather handbags and belts on one stall, cheap t-shirts and baseball caps on another, and costume jewelry on another. Repeated stall after stall, ad infinitum. Not the fresh produce or fish market we had looked forward to, no Spanish pottery or antiques.

One day we visited the high-rise tourist town of Benidorm with Adam, promising him English fish and chips overlooking the amazing blue flag sandy beaches. We spent the day there back in November, the resort full of holidaymakers, the bars packed before noon. After struggling, once more, to find a parking spot big enough for the Mondeo we walked back into town. It was ghostly in comparison to our previous visit. There were a decent number of Spanish tourists, unable to vacation elsewhere, they had flocked to more local resorts. In an attempt to keep tourism and the dependent businesses alive, the beach had been marked out with rope into three-meter square sections. To safely sunbathe and maintain social distancing the ingenious town officials had created an online booking system, where one of the sections could be reserved for the day.

Despite these efforts, the town lacked the gritty downbeat vibe of the rampant British and Scandinavian partygoers who gave rowdy life and noise to the numerous bars along its seafront. Many of the businesses had shuttered, their market taken away by the virus and the Government imposed bans on travel. We walked along the road by the beach for miles in the blistering heat and then finally, without either chips or fish, we gave up and retraced our steps back to the car.

The sunsets were breathtakingly beautiful. The Sierra de Bernia mountain range was a constant backdrop to our time in Altea, especially at twilight when it became a natural canvas, foreshortening the landscape and throwing the fading light back, burnt spice, and burnished copper into the sky. Then nightfall. A darkness for a moment profound and unsullied by the artificial lights of streets and houses until the Milky Way became a blaze above. The valley across from us was unlit and indistinct and the villa felt terribly lonely and isolated at night. A single dog would send out an alarm, and suddenly the darkness between us and the sea would be alive with the barking of the valley's sentinels until the dogs slowly settled once more into silence. I will always remember that fondly as the definitive sound of Spain.

The scenery never stopped being an amazement. Trapped between the mountains and the sea, we looked endlessly in head-shaking wonder at its natural beauty. Living by the Mediterranean, what's not to like? A dream come true, right? Nonetheless, as the days passed and turned into weeks, the extraordinary turned into the mundane. We spent much of our time playing in the pool. We found some wooden bats and small balls in an old wooden chest under the veranda by the pool. Jim had placed all of his family's beach stuff in there for storage, old tennis racquets, pool floats, and beach chairs. Like the house, most of the items he had hoarded away were broken or rusted and beyond use. We spent hours playing a game we called 'bitty batty' a kind of piggy in the middle, one of us trying to catch the ball being hit back and forth from one end of the pool to the other.

The truth was that we were slowly becoming discontent. The weather was wonderful for a vacation, but the relentless heat of this Spanish summer seemed interminable. The dogs had barely left the house in weeks. Our dream, back in America, of perhaps jogging down to the beach and enjoying a coffee and a churro by the Sea was unrealistic. If not that, what were we doing here?

Then, more dark clouds appeared on the horizon to our north. The outbreak and subsequent quarantine we had skirted around in the city of Lleida had not been contained. African fruit pickers, temporary workers from nearby Algeria and Morocco, were still moving across the countryside looking for work and spreading the disease, from the province of Aragon to Catalonia and beyond. The number of infected cases was rising exponentially, up from just over seven hundred a day when we arrived at the villa, the number was now in excess of three thousand a day. Government sabers were being verbally rattled in France and the United Kingdom.

In more normal times, the European Union had implemented the admirable philosophy of free movement for both its citizens and for the goods they produced. It was, of course, now the antithesis of controlling the spread of the highly contagious virus. France was threatening to re-close the land border, trapping us in Spain. A country we were not certain we wanted to be in, not at that time. Britain was talking about restricting travel from the continent once again. The virus had changed life all over the world, seldom for the better and Spain was no exception. Its economy was reeling, businesses were closing and everything that we had looked forward to back in America was gone, at least temporarily.

We thought once more of all of the seasonal markets, festivals, and fiestas we had anticipated visiting when we first dreamt our dream of our new life in Spain, living between the mountains and the Mediterranean. The Christmas markets, the festival of the Fallas in Valencia, the tomato throwing at La Tomatina, or the rockets and wine drinking at the celebration of the Entrà de la Murta. Endless warm nights of celebration, fireworks, and dancing under the stars of a Spanish sky. They were all absent, all paused for the moment, perhaps never to return.

Perpignan

July 28th, 2020

    Perpignan in the evening rush hour. We had been driving in circles for forty minutes and just could not find the Airbnb. Paula specifically booked only properties with private parking and despite being inundated with photos of the apartment from the owner we just couldn't seem to find the damn thing. When booking this one Paula had mistakenly thought that Perpignan would be a small and charming French town with easy access from the autoroute to both the Airbnb and the veterinarian's office we needed to find the next day. I should have taken more notice as I had visited it many years before and knew the city of Perpignan to be a large and sprawling urbanization, home to 220,000 people.

    We were absolutely exhausted from the unbearable nine-hour scorching heat and confinement of the car. The big Mondeo was overheating once more, and poor Archie and Pi were panting, stressed again on the rear seats. Paula finally managed to speak to the owner in a mishmash of broken French and English, who revealed that there was no private parking and instead, we needed to head to the underground parking Clemencau lot on Avenue Marechal Leclerc. We retraced our steps and descended into the garage, shoe-horned the car into a tiny parking spot, and finally, in the suffocating heat of the subterranean lot, the Mondeo gave up, steam billowed from the engine compartment, and hot purple coolant spewed across the concrete floor of the garage.

    We drew quite the crowd but there was nothing to be done at that moment. We needed to take care of ourselves and the puppies. We needed to just find the apartment and get the Pi and Archie cooled and watered. We grabbed the essentials we would need for the night, food, warm beer, and passports, and laden down, we escaped the parking garage into the light and heat of that late afternoon. With each booking of that apartment, the lucky recipient also received an impromptu course in orienteering. Google Maps was telling us that the apartment was still a few hundred yards away. Past Le Théâtre de l'Archipel, across busy intersections we dragged the dogs and baggage, sweaty and bedraggled, we resembled homeless people looking for a bus stop or doorway to sleep in. Finally, we found the apartment on the Avenue de Grande Bretagne and only needed to retrieve the key. Instead of a lockbox by the door, this genius had chained the lockbox to a tree in the middle of a busy traffic island. Like a real-life version of the TV game show Challenge Anneka, we used a photograph he sent to Paula's phone earlier, to match the tree to the one in the picture. Paula sprinted across traffic to the island, returned with the key and we were in.

On Sunday morning, three days earlier, the 26th of July, we woke in the villa, excited to be flying back to the UK for a few days to look at rental properties in Somerset in the South-West of England. We had slowly come to terms with the fact that Spain, at this time, in the middle of this pandemic was not the right place for us. We had decided on Somerset because...well, because we had a pin and a map. Neither of us had ever visited, but it was rural which appealed, with a southern climate and close to Paula's sister Kaz.

We figured we would use our remaining few months at the Villa, turning the time into an extended Spanish vacation, doing some sightseeing and playing in the pool. Then take our time driving slowly through France back to the UK and renting there for a year while we figured out our next steps. Our flight from Alicante to Bristol was at eleven o'clock so I was up early making tea downstairs and checking the BBC website for the latest news.

While we slept, and without warning, the UK Government had imposed an immediate quarantine for visitors arriving from Spain. I spent the day on the phone canceling flights, rental cars, and hotels. The property rental companies we had arranged viewings with all canceled on us. Everybody was once more wary of the rising cases in Spain, and by definition, anybody arriving from the region.

Worse news came from France. The French Government had escalated the rhetoric and was threatening once again to close the land border with Spain. I don't know, in hindsight, if we were too hasty in our decisions at that point. We had little data to go on, but it all pointed to the fact that a second wave was already rising and that we would soon be stranded in a country once more isolated by Europe and locked down by its own Government under a new state of alarm.

The UK had previously closed its borders rapidly and without notice. The dog's original paperwork for international travel would expire within a few months, and with Brexit talks breaking down, the situation was becoming increasingly tenuous.

With the pending threat of the French closing the land border with Spain, we made a decision. We would run for it. A fast sprint to France, and then onward to the relative safety and security of England. Hopefully staying at least one step ahead of the border restrictions.

On Tuesday, the morning of the 28th, we put Adam in a taxi to Alicante airport. He would take the easy route back to Manchester, and then onward to family in Southport in the North-West of England. This would free up room in the car for our journey back across Europe. As soon as Adam was safely on his way, we finished loading the Mondeo and drove out of the villa gates for the last time. Neither I nor Paula gave a second thought or backward glance, which perhaps speaks to the regard in which we held the place. We had a long day ahead of us, nearly four hundred and fifty hot and grueling miles lay between us and Perpignan, just North of the French border.

Bags of ice had been purchased the night before, and we lay these on the back seats with blankets over, in an attempt to keep the dogs cool. I had bought a portable air conditioner that plugged into the car's 12V outlet. It cooled the car, not at all, but it generated the slightest zephyr of a breeze and moved the scorching air around the car. Archie appreciated it and lay in the back, panting, his black muzzle directed toward it. Paula had to constantly keep it topped up with water and it distracted her a little from how we were all suffering in that suffocating oven of a car, heated relentlessly by the torrid Spanish sun that tracked our path northward along the Mediterranean coast. We sweated the miles away, constantly parched and miserable, mile after sultry wretched mile. We hoped more Northern latitudes would help but even the foothills of the Pyrenees refused to offer any relief.

We anxiously crossed into France at Le Perthus, the familiar shadow of the Pyrenees in the distance to our left. The land border was still open, but there was a lot of unusual activity there. Traffic slowed through what looked like a police checkpoint that was being put in place. But nobody we saw was stopped or questioned. And then onward to Perpignan.

Sennely

July 29th, 2020

The Perpignan rental was crappy, and we didn't sleep well, tossing and turning, both worried about the car, abandoned last night in the parking garage. Would it even start in the morning? The night before we had tried to make dinner, but the power in the apartment kept tripping so we ate cold soup and drank a warm beer each.

Paula made a morning coffee for me in the only mug we could find in the grubby kitchen, chasing cockroaches into hiding as she searched for utensils. I took a bite of a meat pie I had brought from Spain, but when I offered the dogs a morsel, Pi balked and Archie looked queasy, making me in turn gag and spit the remainder into the trash. And so, with that hearty breakfast complete, I walked despondently back to the subterranean car park in the watery morning sunshine. Paula took the time to pack our belongings and walk the dogs. The car was exactly as we had left it, standing in a broad vivid purple pool of its own coolant. To my surprise, it started on the first turn of the key, and I drove it tentatively back to the apartment, parking on the pavement outside to finish packing. It was early, still cool and the city was yet to wake. Not one of us wanted to get back into the Mondeo, and another stiflingly sweaty day's drive, but we needed to be at a veterinarian's office in the seaside town of Argeles-sur-Mer. When making the appointment for a worming treatment the dogs would need to allow entry back into the UK, Paula thought the town was walking distance to Perpignan itself, but it was an hour's drive away, in the wrong direction.

The town of Argeles-sur-Mur and the vet, Monsieur Bontemps, were both charmingly French. We found a large, free, and mostly empty parking spot behind the modern sports center in the center of the small town, and walked between some houses toward the veterinarian's office. Monsieur Bontemps arrived at the office at the same time as us, he riding an antiquated black-framed bicycle, a perfect stereotype in his black waistcoat and bicycle clips. He had been recommended to us as he spoke English, which was almost true. True at least in the same manner that I am fluent in Cantonese and Gujarati.

Despite the language challenges, we got the dogs pilled and their paperwork stamped. This part of France was taking a typically Gallic shoulder shrug of an effort to contain the virus. The streets were busy with shoppers and the road to the beaches was packed with holidaymakers, laughing and coughing, carefree in the sunshine of Southern France.

We got lost following Google map instructions to a petrol station that didn't seem to have ever existed so headed back toward Perpignan. We stopped on the outskirts of the city for gas and refilled the car with coolant, putting two spare bottles in the back, just in case, and then we were back on the road heading North. We wanted to get just south of Paris, so we faced another seven hours in that awful oven of a car. If only we had taken an extra day or two in England to get the air conditioning fixed. But that was at the start of the journey, and we never intended to use the car beyond a one-way trip to Spain.

The morning drive took us north and east close to the Mediterranean, adjacent to the vast dark aquamarine salt lagoons on the outskirts of Narbonne. We climbed steadily through the Haut Languedoc region and then through the Massif-Central. Paula tried her best to keep us all from overheating, dampening my brow and the back of my neck, and constantly sprinkling the dogs with cold water as we went. The Mondeo struggled on some of the longer climbs, the temperature gauge moving slowly toward the red, but cooled again as soon as we dropped back into valleys. Huge farms of wind turbines roiled across the hills on both sides of the road. A thousand triads of white blades brushed the clouds across the sky in an outlandish and alien panorama.

The Viaduc de Millau carried us across the gorge valley of the river Tarn at a vertiginous eleven hundred feet, I felt dizzy glancing at the mist that obscured the valley and river below. One of the greatest engineering achievements to date and still the highest bridge in the world, it superseded the record from the Viaduc de Verrieres over the Lumensonesque river which we crossed thirty minutes later. The countryside north of Clermont-Ferrand changed from deep valleys and lofty peaks to rolling farmland, verdant patchwork quilts redolent of England. We left the autoroute close to the small and unremarkable town of Salbris and drove on past small white houses with steeply pitched orange-tiled houses on large-grassed lots toward Sennely, and the welcome end of the day's journey.

By late afternoon we found our house for the evening. A squat brick terrace close to La Chez Fanny, I shit you not, a charming but closed Boulangerie in the sleepy backwater of Sennely, home to only seven-hundred people and notable only for having a chapter dedicated to it in George Huppert's book on social history, "After the Black Death."

The house, however, was perfect, with a large garden and clean kitchen. The neighbor's garden was smaller but full of free-range Bresse Gauloise chickens, snowy white with red combs, they clucked alarm when they saw the dogs, startling and fascinating Archie and making Pi bristle and curl her lips to show all of her five crooked and pointy teeth. We showered ourselves cool and walked the dogs around the village. Another quintessentially French location. It's amazing how France has managed to retain so many places like this, seemingly untouched since the seventeenth century. All despite taking a lead role in staging a significant part of two world wars, and according to George Huppert, an unhealthy dose of the Plague.

We were all, at least for the moment, cool, content, and fed and headed upstairs to the bedroom that looked out over the cobbled street, tiled roofs, and the spire and bell tower of the Eglise Saint-Jean-Baptiste.

A Return to Paris

July 30th, 2020

The morning had started well. The road out of Sennely was a straight and natural tree-lined tunnel of Larch and Cedar. Through gaps in the trees, we could see the occasional tumbledown farmhouse floating serenely on an ocean of golden, waving barley. We passed through the sleepy villages of Marcilly-en-Villette and Saint-Cyr-en-Val. Rustic and rural remnants, throwbacks from a different time, old men straight out of central casting, smoking Gauloises and drinking coffee outside the local Tabac.

France really is beautiful. In the past, for me, it was always a country to transit rather than visit, a race down the Autoroute de Soleil to get to the South or beyond its borders. We both agreed that, should we ever travel again (which seemed highly unlikely at that precise moment), rural Northern France would be on our list of destinations.

We crossed the Loire close to the city of Orleans, shallow water rippled and eddied across sandbanks. We looked down with envious eyes at the kayakers dipping paddles in the sparkling water, enjoying the cool of the broad river. North of Orleans we saw a sign for the town of Saran, our first stop on the trip south to Spain and we are back on familiar roads, re-tracing our steps but now heading north, back toward Paris and the ever-increasing volume and jam of the traffic.

We saw signs for Orly Airport and made the turn onto the Peripherique Est and immediately traffic slowed and then ground to a snarling halt as we approached the Seine. Blistering steam began to rise from the engine compartment and the needle on the temperature gauge of the aging Ford Mondeo crept relentlessly, dangerously once more into the red. The car slowed as we began to lose power and in the rear-view mirror, I could see a purple slick of coolant bleeding onto the searing asphalt behind us. Now here we were, back at the beginning of the story, broken down by the side of the Peripherique, on the Rue Barbes insight of the Moulin de la Tour.

Congestion on the Boulevard Peripherique Est had, if anything, increased. We could still see the melee and hear the clamor of horns from where we were parked. It had taken thirty minutes for the Mondeo to cool sufficiently to risk removing the cap of the coolant reservoir. I checked Google Maps for traffic. The eastbound Peripherique was still jammed close to the narrow crossing over the Seine, but clockwise traffic looked lighter. The western route of the Peripherique is a much longer way around Paris, but if we could keep moving, the car might still get us to the coast.

The car took a surprisingly small amount of replacement coolant and reluctantly we all jumped back into the baking hot car. I really, really, desperately needed the Mondeo to start. In the panic of the rush to leave Spain, I foolishly and recklessly neglected to take out any breakdown insurance. We were alone the two of us, without friends or language in a foreign country, the bad situation could quickly become desperate.

With my fingers crossed, I turned the ignition. The starter motor spun but the engine remained silent. I sat, eyes closed for a slow count of one hundred, and tried once more. The engine turned over but still refused to start. I pinched the bridge of my nose and wiped the sweat from my eyes, and on the third try, with a huge sigh of relief, the car roared back into life.

The traffic was heavy to be sure, but most of the time we were at least moving, inching slowly forward. As traffic slowed, the needle of the temperature gauge crept up. Paula leaned across from the passenger seat to stare at it intently.

"It's going up again, it's going up again," high pitched and desperate with concern, over and over in my ear. I did actually know it was going up. My attention was equally divided by the road ahead and where that bloody needle pointed. In the end, I had to ask her to be quiet, not something a happily married man can get away with very often but being repeatedly told we were on the verge of breaking down really wasn't lessening my stress levels.

With each passing mile, the amount of traffic dropped and our average speed increased, and then finally, hot and with nerves that positively jangled, we were finally off the Peripherique for the last time. We crossed the Seine north of the city, wide and busy with colossal, dark floating barges, carrying industry and fuel to the port of Le Havre on the English Channel, one hundred and fifty miles to the northwest. Our course was to Calais, almost due North and still over three hours distant.

Paula had another Airbnb reserved in Northern France for that evening, but it was still relatively early so we canceled, and Paula called the Channel Tunnel booking office to see if we could get an earlier train. With the UK quarantine now back in place and travel still limited across the continent, there was plenty of space, so we pressed on. Afternoon sunshine was once again making the inside of the car miserable and oppressive. Dogs panting, sweat streaming down the back of my shirt, we all struggled to remain hydrated in the stifling conditions. We seemed to have developed a knack for only traveling on days when daytime temperatures set record-new highs. Paula resumed her role of sprinkling me and the dogs with cold water and topping up the hugely ineffective air conditioner wedged between the two front seats.

The autoroute brought us close to the coast as we passed Boulogne-Sur-Mer and as we crested a hill, the south coast of England was suddenly, surprisingly ahead of us, chalk white and welcoming across the narrow glittering blue straight of the channel. It was a flag of hope that we might yet make it, briefly glimpsed before it was consumed and hidden by the rolling hills and valleys we navigated.

In Calais, the English border guard gave us a hard time when he saw the Spanish registration plates on the car, but Paula had been honest about our place of origin on the passenger locater forms, and being British citizens, he had no choice but to finally and grumpily wave us through. We finally figured out where we needed to go to get the dog's paperwork certified for entry to the UK, and then we were back in the queue for the train back to England.

I had to turn the engine off to keep it as cool as I could as the queue moved slowly forward, waiting until the last minute before I anxiously fired it back into life. We carefully boarded the train and drove down the carriage to take our allotted space in line. With a nod from the guard, I turned the engine off. Thirty-five minutes later, at the end of the channel transit, and hugely relieved when the Mondeo started again, we drove off the train and were back in England.

We made a last-minute booking at a pet-friendly hotel, the Conningbrook on Canterbury Road in Ashford, just a few miles from where the channel tunnel exits onto the M20 outside Folkstone. After a cold shower and a change of clothes, with the dogs fed and settled into the room, we popped into the bar/restaurant attached to the hotel. We found a table and we sat in stunned silence.

The day had been hellish. Close to four hundred miles including our diversion around Paris, close to eight hours stuck in that nightmarish crematorium of a car. We were exhausted, stressed, and de-hydrated. My head pounded from the prolonged heat and my hands still trembled from the worry of the Mondeo just giving out on us and stranding us, the poor dogs, and our meager belongings by the side of some French road in the middle of bum fuck nowhere, or "putain de cul nulle part," as they say in those Gallic parts.

We sat quietly, staring into the middle distance, contemplating all of the things that had and might have gone wrong, and how lucky we had been to beat the impending lockdown of frontiers and the seemingly inevitable breakdown of that bloody car.

As we sat there, a chirpy young server came by to take our drinks order.

"How's your day been?" he politely asked.

Southport

July 31st, 2020

We reunited with Adam in Southport the next day. The car overheated twice more on that short journey forcing us to break the journey and find a place to wait for it to cool sufficiently so I could add more coolant. The last time was in the middle of Ormskirk, a frustratingly trifling eight miles from our final destination of Southport.

The traffic all day had been awful, start-stop queues every mile, from the south of England to the North-West. Tell me, where were all these people going? The country was still supposed to be in lockdown. As we pulled into the market town, traffic slowed and Paula leaned across me to watch, stricken as the needle of the temperature gauge slipped once more into the danger zone. The Mondeo was steaming and losing coolant again so we had to pull out of the long queue of traffic that was crawling up the steep hill that leads out of the busy town.

We found a spot in a cramped car park in the small shopping center opposite the public swimming baths. We did our usual routine, I popped the bonnet of the car to facilitate additional cooling, and Paula watered and then walked the dogs on a small patch of dandelion-covered grass by the shops. If you ever need to summon the attention of, and subsequently amuse, a large group of strangers, park a really hot car in a crowded car park. Works every time. With the Mondeo cooling, we risked setting off once more. The car was still piled high with Archie and Pi and all of our possessions. All now jumbled and carelessly strewn, thrown into whatever space we could find, nothing benefitting from the constant packing and unpacking of the journey. I couldn't see out the back of the Mondeo at all and, of course, I had disconnected the parking sensors back in Spain. I backed carelessly, loudly, and crunchingly into a cast iron bollard that creased the back of the increasingly shabby and dilapidated Mondeo.

Over three thousand miles, we had driven, to Spain and back, and here we were, emotionally spent, eight miles from our goal. We were hot and tired and close to tears, but we were desperately close to the finish line, so we took some deep breaths, maneuvered with a little more care out of the car park, and took a back route out of town, longer but with less snarled summer traffic and onward to Southport.

We had to quarantine again (thanks Boris), Paula's eldest sister Janice, thankfully lent us her house in which to do so. Janice and her family were vacationing at their caravan in Wales, so the house was vacant. The morning we had set off from the villa four days prior, Adam had flown from Alicante to Manchester and was waiting at the house to let us in.

Southport is our hometown the place where both Paula and I were born, went to school together, and grew up. I may forget some of the street names, and now and again the road junctions will change, but I know it intimately. We drove the familiar streets, over the hill that takes traffic over Meols cop train station, past Emmanuel church, and down the quiet street where Janice lives, cars parked on either side, like almost every other urban street in England. Pulling up to the house we backed the big Mondeo up the drive. Turning the ignition off we sat in silence for a full minute and looked at each other with relief. The journey back had been a brutal adventure, the last two days a nightmare, at times despairing that we would ever make it back safely.

We unloaded the dogs, wondering why Adam hadn't already opened the door. We had texted him that morning as we left Ashford and he had texted back, so we knew he was expecting us, and we really looked forward to our reunion, seeing him, and catching up on each other's stories. Banging on the front door still didn't elicit a response. We called his cell phone, no response. I dragged a garbage bin across to the back gate and clumsily jumped over the backyard gate, bruising a knee and gaining the interest of the neighbor. Luckily the back door was open.

I found Adam passed out, drunk on the sofa with a spilling cup of cold coffee in his lap. We were furious, it was only two o'clock in the afternoon and he had known we would be arriving at the end of a four-day journey, but instead of greeting us with smiles, hugs, and perhaps a cold refreshing beer or two, he had chosen to get absolutely blackout pissed. It took us weeks to forgive him.

Second Quarantine

July 31st to August 8th, 2020

England was easy and familiar despite our absence of fourteen years. We still had credit histories, bank cards, and National Insurance and National Health Service numbers, and within days we had working British cell phones. It was the polar opposite of life in Spain, and we were able to walk straight back into our old identities as citizens of this lovely little, green, and rain-sodden island.

I couldn't sell the Mondeo, even for scrap. I called breakers yards by the dozen, but regulations regarding car disposal had been tightened since my departure to the United States. It used to be that a scrap yard or salvage yard would pay cash for any piece of broken-down junk metal, regardless of its provenance or dubious history. The European Union had stopped all that malarky. Lord alone knows what getaway drivers do with hot property these days, but with its Spanish registration and paperwork, the Mondeo was one potato too hot to handle, and I was refused at every turn. I phoned a web-based company called webuyanycar.com only to find out that their proud boast is a lie. It should have been called:

webuyanycarexeptspanishregisteredlefthanddrives.com.

With Janice returning in a few days, I couldn't have the oily, broken down, and now dented Mondeo on her drive. It really was becoming the gift that kept taking, and the clock was ticking.

I was on the internet one afternoon researching how best to commit a crime, just driving the car into the country under cover of the night, leaving the keys in the ignition and setting it alight or just simply walking away, when I stumbled on a forum that recommended not taking that particularly illegal route, but instead donating to a wonderful company called Give a Car. They will literally take any vehicle, including the dodgy piece of crap I called my own, pick it up from your location, either sell or scrap it depending on condition (read scrap) and send any proceeds to a charity of your choice. I chose Cancer research and on the sunny Friday afternoon, after we arrived, the big old blue car and I were parted.

Paula celebrated with bunting and a street party. I was honestly more mixed. It had been an awful, dreadful car to drive in the extreme heat, cruel to both us, and the poor dogs, but that was all my fault for buying it both unseen and untested, and subsequently not taking the time to have the air conditioning repaired. Otherwise, it had driven beautifully, been most economical, and ultimately got us both to our dream and back safely.

The very next day we visited Oldfield's, an old family-owned car dealership just outside the town center, one my dad had frequented when I was growing up. In 1975, when I was ten years old, he bought a tiny mustard-colored Mini from them, with the registration plate TOF 65N. I still remember fondly heading up to Scotland in it for a vacation. Mum and Dad were in the front, Dad driving, me and my brother Dave sat in the back squabbling. We bought a similarly tiny, bright red Hyundai, from the son of the man who had sold the Mini to my Dad all those years ago. It started and ran beautifully. Paula had recently developed a nervous tick on our journey across Europe, constantly glancing across at the temperature gauge, brow furrowed; it took almost two years for it to go away completely. The needle on the Hyundai never moved once the engine was warmed, it even had air conditioning, which, of course, now we were back in England we never used.

Adam went out in the morning and walked the streets of the town trying to find employment. Southport has changed every year we returned on visits from the USA. A little shabbier and downbeat each time. Most of the large department stores have gone, replaced by charity or coffee shops. Debenhams, Woolworths, and Broadbent's, all massive outlets and employers in the town, proud legacies of the town's once-booming Victorian heritage, closed or broken into smaller and tackier retail units. My Mum had been the Human Resources Manager at Debenhams, and it hurt just to see the store she loved, now missing from the broad tree-lined boulevards of Lord Street. The same street is said to have inspired the boulevards of Paris after Prince Louis-Napoléon Bonaparte, the future Napoléon III lived just off Lord Street in 1846.

Jobs were few and hard to find. Most employers had furloughed staff during the early days of the pandemic, and even if business picked back up, they intended to re-hire those employees ahead of any new applicants. We visited letting agencies with Adam to try and locate a flat or an apartment where he could live. The situation with the apartments was even more dire, there was zero availability and nothing on the market.

Paula and I rented a cottage in Somerset, obviously without seeing it, because that's who we had become. It was one of the properties we had intended to view when our trip to the UK from Spain had been curtailed, all the way back on that Sunday morning only a few days prior. It was in the village of Somerton, the monthly rent was reassuringly expensive, and the location and pictures represented it well, how bad could it be? Recognize any obvious patterns or mistakes to be repeated yet? Our rental period was for one year and would start on August 10th, only a few days away.

We visited with Adrian, my old friend, and Caroline one of Paula's best friends, enjoying dinner and drinks in the Hesketh Arms in the old town of Churchtown, adjacent to Southport. We had dinner with more friends, Sue and John, driving up to their lovely house located in Up Holland. We took the little Hyundai to give it a test drive. Friends who always took the time to visit us no matter how many years we had been absent. Friends who had made the considerable effort to visit us when we were in Atlanta.

And then our time in Southport was over. Tomorrow, on Sunday afternoon, we three, me, Paula, and Adam would drive down to a hotel near Somerton, ready for another new life in Somerset. Adam had decided to accompany us to Somerset to see if the rural towns of the South offered more prospects. At least he would have a place to live.

Somerset

August 9th, 2020

    Back to packing the car, this time the little Hyundai. Paula had cleverly located a courier company called Sherpa with whom she had arranged to pick up the bulk of our possessions from Janice's house and have them delivered at the rental in Somerton a day after we arrived. I harbored some concerns with Adam accompanying us to the rural backwater that is Somerset. I felt that we had influenced his decision to leave the US, and now we were dragging him away from Southport as well. We chatted, and at the eleventh hour, he finally agreed to stay and continue his quest to find employment and accommodation, at least for a few more weeks, at which point we would re-evaluate options. We found and booked a cheap hotel in town for him, said our goodbyes once more, promised to keep in regular contact, and around noon we drove away from him and Southport.

    We couldn't get the keys to the rental cottage until the following day, so we were headed to a country pub that was dog-friendly and still open for accommodation. The motorway was congested, and we were diverted off the M5 in Birmingham due to an accident, but we still made reasonable time and pulled up in the car park behind the Halfway House in time for dinner. The hotel was old and oak-beamed, with a large lake behind the car park. The accommodation was located in the courtyard, small but comfortable rooms with access directly from the courtyard itself, perfect for Archie and Pi. With the dogs fed and watered, we ate a pub meal in the small restaurant and then retired to sit beside the lake, with the pups and a couple of cold beers, and watched the sun fade behind the sheep-speckled hills in the distance.

    We woke early, excited to see, for the first time, the cottage we had rented for a year. Skipping the breakfast we had bought with the room, Paula drove us to Somerton. The roads were narrow and twisting, lined by tall hedgerows that obscured the views. This part of the world was new to us, but it was definitively England, countryside with rich farmland, a pleasing mix of arable and pastoral, expansive fields rolling into the distance with gentle hills topped by coppice and woodland.

As we pulled into the village of Somerton we were delighted. Rows of ham stone honey-colored cottages greeted us with sagging crowns of rickety red tile or aging thatch, and the flag of St. George waved welcome from the crenelated roof of the thirteenth-century church of St. Michaels. Our rental cottage too was a delight. The key had been quaintly and trustfully left under a stone by the front door and the cottage was a clever combination of traditional and modern, all at the same time. Every appliance in the kitchen was brand new and the two bathrooms had been tastefully and beautifully updated. The location was perfect, right in the middle of the village, close to pubs, a small supermarket, and a real old English butcher's shop selling back bacon and juicy lamb chops.

There was a pleasant walled garden in the rear with seating and double French doors that lead back into the cottage. A grassed area was located to the front, a dilapidated wooden gate kept the dogs from straying onto the quiet road. We unpacked the car and stowed our few things. In the afternoon we went shopping in the busier town of Yeovil (Yeo-vile to the locals, with good reason), to get basics, cutlery, utensils, and groceries to stock the refrigerator. It seemed that at last we had lucked out, and fallen on our feet. There were precisely two too many couches for the space, but it was the opposite of the Spanish villa, a good place to be until we decided on our next steps.

New Horizons

Christmas 2020

Adam did his best to look for work and a more permanent place to live, but ultimately there was nothing available for him in Southport. He was quickly burning through his savings and the small amount of cash we had provided. He had interviews, but no offers of employment were made. All employers were quite rightly prioritizing the re-hire of workers they had been forced to furlough earlier in the year. There wasn't even a long-term room in the first accommodation he stayed in, and he had to move from one seedy hotel to another, again and again. Each time packing, then dragging his belongings to a coffee shop and sitting there, lonely, waiting for the new empty, squalid room to become available. We chatted with Adam on a Saturday evening, the night before our twenty-ninth wedding anniversary, on August 23rd. He was despondent and alone, and I offered to drive back to Southport on our anniversary to pick him up and bring him back to Somerton.

I set off before dawn the next day, putting our anniversary sushi dinner plans on hold. Before I set off, I gave Paula her gift, a framed photo collage I had printed of our favorite pictures of Tybee, our beloved Labrador we had left behind. The nine-hour round trip was rainy but uneventful. I picked him up outside the once esteemed and expensive Prince of Wales Hotel on Lord Street. The hotel is now vainglorious, a bleak and shabby reminder of its elegant past, with outdated rooms and broken windows that admitted pigeons to shit on the carpets in the halls.

He looked tired and sad, defeated. We hugged hello and drove to a dispiriting McDonalds on the Promenade where we had a piping hot coffee, overlooking the endless scrubby and muddy sands Southport calls a beach. We picked up his X-Box from his cousin's house and set off back to Somerton.

He spent some time with us in the village, laughing together, recalling our misadventures, and drinking cider in the White Hart and Unicorn pubs. We got lunch in the city of Wells when Kaz and Steve came for a visit. Wells is famous for its claim to be the smallest city in England, the impressive thirteenth-century cathedral, and it being the location for the film Hot Fuzz. We watched the film that night, pointing out the now-familiar locations used in the film. He came with us on our muddy dog walks, across the fields behind the cottage.

It was great to have him around, a few twenty-year-old mistakes aside, he is a wonderful person, hard-working, funny to be around, and full of joy. But he had made his mind up, England was not the right place for him. He had decided to return to the United States. His friend Bob had offered to loan him a place on a sofa in an apartment back in Roswell. So, a few weeks later, on the 14th of September, we hugged him hard, failed to hold back tears, and said our farewells once more. We waved as the car pulled away, craning our necks to keep him in view for as long as we could until the car turned a corner and took him from us, destined for Heathrow, to catch the flight back to the place that was really always his home.

At the time of writing, a few days before Christmas, waiting for 2021, Paula and I are still here, watching the English weather shift toward winter, and waiting for the pubs to open from yet another British COVID lockdown. We looked into buying a house here in the British country, amid the rolling hills and charming apple orchards of the Somerset countryside. It is a place Archie and Pi adore, it is cool, with long, and frequently damp walks across the fields and through leafy woodlands. We viewed a number of properties, here in Somerset and neighboring Dorset and Devon. We even went as far as making offers on two houses, but ultimately, we backed out of both. This place, this time, this sleepy quiet country village life, not what we both wanted at that point in our lives.

And so, after such a long and difficult journey, we had reached our dream in Spain, only to discover it to be not what we were in search of. Was it all, at the end of everything simply a failure, a waste of time and effort? We look at the time instead as an adventure, a joint-life experience to be savored, remembered together by the three of us. It has lent clarity and shaped our outlook on life and the future in a way only a joint struggle and a dream not quite realized can. From the remote distance of four thousand miles, we had looked forward to seeing more of the family we had left behind in England, picking up from where we had left perhaps. With only a few exceptions, the combination of years passed, and our prolonged separation has put a point of division and detachment between us, a virtual gap in life experiences that seems difficult to bridge.

We are looking forward to our first British Christmas here in fourteen years, close to Kaz and Steve and warm beer and pork pies. When Spring arrives, however, we have decided to leave this place and return to the United States, return to be close again to Ben and Adam and all of our American friends. It has been a decision that took us both a little by surprise, it snuck up on us at different times. We have to constantly remind ourselves, living in this village idyll, and safe and drippy countryside, that this was never the plan. England was a safe haven, a refuge, and a place of sanctuary in the storm of closing borders that surrounded us when we fled Spain.

If COVID restrictions allow, in March, I will return with my wife and best friend, my co-conspirator and adventurer to Atlanta. We will build a new life, and pursue a new dream. We have much of the United States still to explore, and now we have the time to travel and look for a new home, perhaps a place in the country, with chickens and lots of Labradors.

Thank you so much for the read—it is genuinely appreciated. If you enjoyed the tale, it would be very kind of you to leave a review on your favorite bookstore.

Please take a moment to visit my website to see more books and get great discounts and offers.

You can find me at www.andycwareing.com
ANDY C WAREING

Read the next books in the series:
WE'RE ON OUR WAY

IT'S NOT AS BAD AS IT LOOKS

ANDY C WAREING

Andy is a multi-genre Indie author, originally from the United Kingdom. He has lived with his wife Paula and their two dogs Archie and Pi in Atlanta GA for the last fifteen years (with the exception of a year in Spain/UK during the pandemic). At heart always British, he loved living in the U.S.A but will never vocalize the American pronunciations of basil, banana, or tomato. He currently lives in leafy Somerset, land of apples, cider, and weather so perpetually wet, 'wellies' are considered formal wear.

Please take a moment to visit my website to see more books and get great discounts and offers.

You can find me at www.andycwareing.com

ANDY C WAREING

Be a stalker and follow me on Facebook, Goodreads, or my author page on Amazon for updates on new projects:

f
facebook.com/andycwareing

g
goodreads.com/author/show/21017809.Andy_C_Wareing

a
amazon.com/author/andycwareing

email: author@andycwareing.com

Printed in Great Britain
by Amazon